Prepare for the Great Tribulation and the Era of Peace

Prepare for the Great Tribulation and the Era of Peace

Volume X:
January 1, 1998 – March 31, 1998

by John Leary

PUBLISHING COMPANY
P.O. Box 42028 Santa Barbara, CA 93140-2028
(800) 647-9882 • (805) 957-4893 • Fax: (805) 957-1631

The publisher recognizes and accepts that the final authority regarding these apparitions and messages rests with the Holy See of Rome, to whose judgement we willingly submit.

– The Publisher

Cover art by Josyp Terelya

©1998 Queenship Publishing

Library of Congress Number # 95-73237

Published by:
 Queenship Publishing
 P.O. Box 42028
 Santa Barbara, CA 93140-2028
 (800) 647-9882 • (805) 957-4893 • Fax: (805) 957-1631

Printed in the United States of America

ISBN: 1-57918-073-6

Acknowledgments

It is in a spirit of deep gratitude that I would like to acknowledge first the Holy Trinity: Father, Jesus, and the Holy Spirit, the Blessed Virgin Mary and the many saints and angels who have made this book possible.

My wife, Carol, has been an invaluable partner. Her complete support of faith and prayers has allowed us to work as a team. This was especially true in the many hours of indexing and proofing of the manuscript. All of our family has been a source of care and support.

I am greatly indebted to Josyp Terelya for his very gracious offer to provide the art work for this publication. He has spent three months of work and prayer to provide us with a selection of many original pictures. He wanted very much to enhance the visions and messages with these beautiful and provocative works. You will experience some of them throughout these volumes.

A very special thank you goes to my spiritual director, Fr. Leo J. Klem, C.S.B. No matter what hour I called him, he was always there with his confident wisdom, guidance and discernment. His love, humility, deep faith and trust are a true inspiration.

My appreciation also goes to Father John V. Rosse, my good pastor at Holy Name of Jesus Church. He has been open, loving and supportive from the very beginning.

There are many friends and relatives whose interest, love and prayerful support have been a real gift from God. Our own Wednesday, Monday and First Saturday prayer groups deserve a special thank you for their loyalty and faithfulness.

Finally, I would like to thank Bob and Claire Schaefer of Queenship Publishing for providing the opportunity to bring this message of preparation, love and warnings to you the people of God.

John Leary, Jr.

Dedication

To the Most Holy Trinity

God

The Father, Son and Holy Spirit

The Source of

All

Life, Love and Wisdom

Publisher's Foreword

John has, with some exceptions, been having visions twice a day since they began in July, 1993. The first vision of the day usually takes place during morning Mass, immediately after he receives the Eucharist. If the name of the church is not mentioned, it is a local Rochester, NY, church. When out of town, the church name is included in the text. The second vision occurs in the evening, either at Perpetual Adoration or at the prayer group that is held at Holy Name of Jesus Church.

Various names appear in the text. Most of the time, the names appear only once or twice. Their identity is not important to the message and their reason for being in the text is evident. First names have been used, when requested by the individual.

We are grateful to Josyp Terelya for the cover art, as well as for the art throughout the book. Josyp is a well-known visionary and also, the author of *Witness* and most recently *In the Kingdom of the Spirit*.

This volume covers messages from January 1, 1998 through March 31, 1998. The volumes will now be coming out quarterly due to the urgency of the messages.

Volume I: July, 1993 through June, 1994.
Volume II: July, 1994 through June, 1995.
Volume III: July, 1995 through July 10, 1996.
Volume IV: July 11, 1996 through September 30, 1996.
Volume V: October 1, 1996 through December 31, 1996.
Volume VI: January 1, 1997 through March 31, 1997.
Volume VII: April 1, 1997 through June 30, 1997.
Volume VIII: July 1, 1997 through September 30, 1997.
Volume IX: October 1, 1997 through December 31, 1997.

The Publisher

Foreword

It was in July of 1993 that Almighty God, especially through Jesus, His Eternal Word, entered the life of John Leary in a most remarkable way. John is 55 years old and is a retired chemist from Eastman Kodak Co., Rochester, New York. He lives in a modest house in the suburbs of Rochester with Carol, his wife of thirty-two years, and Catherine, his youngest daughter. His other two daughters, Jeanette and Donna, are married and have homes of their own. John has been going to daily Mass since he was seventeen and has been conducting a weekly prayer group in his own home for twenty-five years. For a long time, he has been saying fifteen decades of the Rosary each day.

In April of 1993 he and his wife made a pilgrimage to Our Lady's shrine in Medjugorje, Yugoslavia. While there, he felt a special attraction to Jesus in the Blessed Sacrament. There he became aware that the Lord Jesus was asking him to change his way of life and to make Him his first priority. A month later in his home, Our Lord spoke to him and asked if he would give over his will to Him to bring about a very special mission. Without knowing clearly to what he was consenting, John, strong in faith and trust, agreed to all the Lord would ask.

On July 21, 1993 the Lord gave him an inkling of what would be involved in this new calling. He was returning home from Toronto in Canada where he had listened to a talk of Maria Esperanza (a visionary from Betania, Venezuela) and had visited Josyp Terelya. While in bed, he had a mysterious interior vision of a newspaper headline that spelled "DISASTER." Thus began a series of daily and often twice daily interior visions along with messages, mostly from Jesus. Other messages were from God the Father, the Holy Spirit, the Blessed Virgin Mary, his guardian angel and many of the saints, especially St. Therese of Lisieux. These messages he recorded on his word processor. In the beginning, they were quite short, but they became more extensive as the weeks passed by. At the time of this writing, he is still receiving visions and messages.

These daily spiritual experiences, which occur most often immediately following Communion, consist of a brief vision which becomes the basis of the message that follows. They range widely on a great variety of subjects, but one might group them under the following categories: warnings, teachings and love messages. Occasionally, there are personal confirmations of some special requests that he made to the Lord.

The interior visions contain an amazing number of different pictures, some quite startling, which hardly repeat themselves. In regard to the explicit messages that are inspired by each vision, they contain deep insights into the kind of relationship God wishes to establish with His human creatures. There, also, is an awareness of how much He loves us and yearns for our response. As a great saint once wrote: "Love is repaid only by love." On the other hand, God is not a fool to be treated lightly. In fact, did not Jesus once say something about not casting pearls before the swine? Thus, there are certain warnings addressed to those who shrug God off as if He did not exist or is not important in human life.

Along with such warnings, we become more conscious of the reality of Satan and the forces of evil "...which wander through the world seeking the ruin of souls." We used to recite this at the end of each low Mass. In His love and concern for us, Our Lord keeps constantly pointing out how frail we humans are in the face of such evil angelic powers. God is speaking of the necessity of daily prayer, of personal penance, and of turning away from atheistic and material enticements which are so much a part of our modern environment.

Perhaps the most controversial parts of the messages are those which deal with what we commonly call Apocalyptic. Unusual as these may be, in my judgment, they are not basically any different than what we find in the last book of the New Testament or in some of the writings of St. Paul. After a careful and prayerful reading of the hundreds of pages in this book, I have not found anything contrary to the authentic teaching authority of the Roman Catholic Church.

The 16th Century Spanish mystic, St. John of the Cross, gives us sound guidelines for discerning the authenticity of this sort of phenomena involving visions, locutions, etc. According to him, there are three possible sources: the devil, some kind of self-imposed hypnosis or God. I have been John's spiritual confidant for over five years. I have tested him in various spiritual ways and I am most confident that all he has put into these messages is neither of the devil nor of some kind of mental illness. Rather, they are from the God who, in His love for us, wishes to reveal His own Divine mind and heart. He has used John for this. I know that John is quite ready to abide by any decision of proper ecclesiastical authority on what he has written in this book.

Rev. Leo J. Klem, C.S.B.
Rochester, New York
1993

Visions and Messages
of John Leary:

Thursday, January 1, 1998: (Solemnity of Mary)
After Communion, I could see Mary briefly holding the Infant Jesus, but I could not see her face. Mary said: *"My dear children, I bring you my Son every time that I visit you. Wherever I am, He is there also. We are inseparable. I rejoice with you in my Son's First Coming and I am always witnessing to my Son's Second Coming as well. You have difficulty seeing my face because I will not be giving you messages much longer. My time of announcement of my Son's Coming again is about to end. The angels will be with you to strengthen you in these end days. Continue to keep my Rosary and my Scapular with you for all the promises of my help to you. Prayer is a way of life that you will need until your dying days. Remember the last words of the Hail Mary... 'now and at the hour of our death.'"*

Later, at St. Rene's Adoration, Troy, Michigan, I could see a book opened on a table. Jesus said: *"My people, many find themselves distracted by too many worldly concerns. To gain a stronger focus on Me, make time in your day for some good spiritual reading. The best source of spiritual reading to start with is the Bible or the writings of the saints. By making a regular commitment to such reading, you will be able to cut through your distractions and see how I can work in your life. I have given you many messages on how to build your spirituality. Take My advice to heart if you really are striving toward perfection in your soul."*

Friday, January 2, 1998:
At Sts. Cyril and Methodius Church, Sterling Heights, Mich., after Communion, I could see a church and Jesus was leading people

down into an underground place. Jesus said: *"My people, I will always be watching over My faithful sheep as a good shepherd. Never fear any of the trials that you will face in the end days because I will be at your side. Even when persecution will force you into an underground church, I will be there to lead you and give you peace. All power resides with Me and these trials are being allowed to strengthen and test your faith. Whoever has faith in Me, they will follow Me even if your life may be threatened. Life in the spirit with Me is your most treasured goal. Never leave My sheepfold or you will surely be lost. My faithful servants will live to see My glory in the renewed earth. Pray constantly so your love for Me will carry you through whatever you have to face in this life. Knowing that I am with you at all times will help you bear any hardship you may suffer."*

Later, at St. Joseph's Church, Erie, Mich. Adoration, I could see some half-moons and many strange lights and stars in the skies. Jesus said: *"My people, do not be influenced by those in astrology or the New Age Movement. The evil one will be cunning with all of his magical signs and illusions. Do not believe any of his lies, but remain faithful in living through this trial. I alone have the most power. Believe in following My Will only and you will be saved. Protect yourself from the evil one's influence with your sacramentals and never worship anyone else but Me. No matter what others will promise you, do not believe their lies. Hold close to Me and your guardian angel and that will be enough to overcome any evil influence. Your faith and perseverence will be rewarded with My Real Presence in Heaven."*

Saturday, January 3, 1998: (Funeral Mass)

At Sts. Cyril and Methodius, Sterling Heights, Mich., after Communion, I could see a man standing in a suit of armor with a shield. Then there was a parade of warriors being welcomed triumphantly. Jesus said: *"My dear people, do not grieve for My faithful who leave this world, for their joy will be complete in Heaven. Your prayer will console those who are grieving the loss of the life that you knew here. Look on the vision of the soldier that I have shown you. During life, My grace gives you the armor to fight the evil one. Each day you must go out and do battle to*

Volume X

witness My Name and My love for all men. Defend your Faith against all who would defile Me and stand up in public to be counted as one of My faithful. Be proud of your heritage in My promise and follow My Will in all that you do. By testifying to My Divine Will, you will gain your crown of eternal life with Me. The vision continues to show you how all of My prayer warriors will be welcomed triumphantly into the Gates of Heaven. You have fought the good race and all of My faithful servants will walk proud in the glory of My Name. Because you have accepted Me as Lord of your life, I will bring you before My Father, for all men must come through Me to enter Heaven."

Sunday, January 4, 1998: (The Epiphany)

At St. Anastasia's Church, Troy, Mich., after Communion, I could see some kings on camels and then a cave. Jesus said: *"My people, I come to you today as the King of the Universe, when the kings of the world gave Me praise long ago. While others realized My Glory, My own Hebrew people tried to kill Me, both when I was born and when I died at the hands of Pilate. My Kingship was a threat to Herod and the Scribes and Pharisees. I was a threat to them because My ways are contrary to the ways of the world. Today, many refuse to accept Me as Lord of their lives, even when I created you and died for you. You are made in My image to give Me praise and glory. See that I am the one who draws your soul to My glory. Man is always desirous to control his own life, even when he fails every time without My help. It is giving your will over to your Master and King that will lead you to My Heavenly Kingdom. You cannot deny My Kingship, you can only refuse it. I am in fact King and I have power over all. I give you free will to accept My love. I am seeking your love at all times. Come to your Master's table and you will share in My glorious banquet and the eternal life that awaits My faithful."*

Later, at Adoration, I could see one plant flourishing and another plant had withered up and died. Jesus said: *"My people, I look at each soul's success in this life from a whole different perspective than yours. Many of you judge someone by how much wealth they have in money and possessions. Others rate how famous someone is on TV, the movies, or by the number of awards that they have acquired. But what is more important in this life — the physical or the spiritual? I judge a person by how much they have loved Me and their neighbor. Each of you stores up spiritual treasures as well as financial treasures. But spiritual treasures are from your good deeds and your prayer life, while financial treasures are those saved for yourself. So, see in My eyes that those things you do for others far outweighs anything that you do selfishly for only you. Let this be a lesson to you in how to prioritize what you are doing. You do far more good for your soul when you do things for Me or others than those you do for yourself. Direct your time, then, in doing more for Me and your neighbor and you will be storing up treasures in Heaven of much more value than the things of earth."*

Monday, January 5, 1998:

After Communion, I could see a dark, circular, rotating donut. Jesus said: *"My people, the day you first believed in Me was the day you became at odds with the world. The evil of the worldly ones denies Me in everything that I do. That is why when you follow My commands, others will question your intentions and actually hate you for trying to be good. They will wonder why you do not cheat and take pleasures like they do. Your lifestyle will in time infuriate others that you are too holy and they will reject you. As the evil Antichrist comes to power, he will declare that you are an outlaw and do not worship him and his gods. That is why you are seeing this dark circulating tunnel. As an outlaw from the evil authorities, they will seek to kill you in an evil religious persecution that you have yet to see. You will be on the run constantly, but do not give in to worship of the Antichrist or take the Mark of the Beast. Keep faithful to Me and I will protect your soul from all evil influence. You will be forced into hiding, but this time of persecution will not last long since I will strike down these evil rulers shortly."*

Later, at Adoration, I could see many houses joined together as one and a great light shown all around them. Jesus said: *"My people, I bring you My love and My peace that it may draw all of you together in My One Mystical Body. Do not let Satan divide you by your pride and cause division amongst My faithful. You need to be united even more now to fight your enemy of the soul in Satan. You all will be faced with persecution for belief in My Name. You will be forced to discern the spirit of all those that speak out in My Name. Those who love Me and teach My laws and love to others will be with you. Those who seek division and spread hate among My faithful will be judged accordingly. So, come to Me in love and forgive each other your own transgressions. I have told you to make amends with your brother before you bring your gift to the altar. Come to Me in Confession to seek the forgiveness of your sins, then My grace and peace will rest on your souls. By following Me in love and love of neighbor, you will be on the right path to Heaven."*

Tuesday, January 6, 1998:
After Communion, I could see a train moving through a tunnel with a light at the end of the tunnel. Jesus said: *"My people, your time of tribulation will be like this train moving through the tunnel. You will have to face the darkness of evil men and the influence of the Antichrist. Your trial will seem much longer than it will be, but that time will be shortened for the sake of the elect. You will suffer much during the tribulation, but I will be guiding you as the tracks for the train. The exit of the tunnel into the light represents My coming in triumph to defeat Satan and my bringing you to My Era of Peace. Once you are completely free of the evil one's influence, you will marvel in My glory and be ever thankful for My many gifts that protected you. A new era of life will open up for you and all of My faithful will reap the reward of their labors. So, have faith and hope in Me but a moment in this trial, and you will share the Heaven on earth that awaits you."*

Later, at Adoration, I could see some new cars coming off the assembly line. Jesus said: *"My people of America, you have become so immersed in your materialism that you do not even realize its influence on you. For many are struggling to have the best houses, cars and electrical conveniences that they can afford. You have become so desirous of these earthly things that most of your time is taken up in acquiring them. You work long hours, even on Sundays, just to satisfy your craving for luxuries. Affluence has spoiled you and many are so distracted by these things that your spiritual lives have gone wanting. When your car does not work or your electricity goes off, you see that you are not always in control. You need to wake up, My friends, and see that there is more to life than your possessions. You need to concern yourself more with helping your neighbor and having a good prayer life. This is the love in life that is missing in your modern* world. Take away your selfish desires of the flesh and replace it with your loving desire to serve Me. You can serve Me best in praising Me in prayer and providing for the needs of your neighbor. When more of your time is spent following My Will, you will be on the right road to your salvation."

Wednesday, January 7, 1998:

After Communion, I could see some large spools of plastic film in a workplace. Jesus said: *"My people, many workers feel like prisoners in their jobs, since they are locked in by circumstances of supporting their families and making ends meet. Even when the workplace is a test, do not lose heart, for I see all of what you are going through. It is enough to be using your hands for My Work and not to feel frustrated that you want more out of life. Many forces of the world seem to be weighing you down, but remember that you are only here as a test of your faith in Me. Being rich in this life is not your goal, but being rich in My treasures is the desire of your soul. So, do not be upset by life's trials, but keep focused on following My Will. You follow My Will when you are obedient to My commands and doing works of mercy. Always be looking to help others and keep focused on Me in your prayer life. I look into the intentions of your soul and I measure your efforts more on how you love, than whether you are financially successful. Look forward to My Day in Glory when My faithful will be rewarded with Heaven on earth. Then your peace will know no end."*

Thursday, January 8, 1998:

After Communion, I could see Jesus on the cross and a bright light shown all around Him. Jesus said: *"My people, this Gospel reading has a profound meaning for why I came into your world. The promise of a Messiah was foretold since Adam's sin. The description of the Holy One who would heal the sick and the blind, and raise the dead, all had to be fulfilled. That is why when I read the scroll of My Coming in the Spirit, I had to announce to all those in My hearing that now the Scriptures have been fulfilled in Me. This is significant because I was sent in answer to the promise for the redemption of all mankind. The light you are* seeing is the witness of the Holy Spirit who moves Me. As the Third Person of the Blessed Trinity, He radiates love in all I do. I am infinite love by the Spirit. That is why My love consumes those who live in My Divine Will. I am in constant search for each soul to bind in an eternal love with Me in the Holy Spirit. I love you no matter how many sins you commit. That is why My forgiveness has no end. But you must come to Me for that forgiveness in Confession. It is by confessing your sins that you are fully restored into My graces. Without the cleansing power of My death on the cross, you could not have your sins forgiven. But I have given you this gift in My sacraments, so come to Me and receive your salvation."*

Later, at the prayer group, I could see a large stained glass window in a church. Jesus said: *"My people, your Mass is under siege from the evil one. Many are trying to implement changes in the Mass that strike at the sacred. Different species of bread and different words throughout the Mass are challenging the validity of My Real Presence at the Consecration. The words I gave My Apostles were My model for My Eucharistic Banquet. Those who do not say the proper words are not saying valid Masses. All that is sacred at Mass must be preserved or you are just going through the motions with no meaning."*

I could see a walled fortress with swords laying on the top of the wall. Jesus said: *"My people, do not take up the sword against each other since war will not settle your disputes. Seek My peace over the whole world and pray that peace may come among all of your factions. It is only by seeking the peace of Christmas that true peace will come among you."*

I could see some electrical leads and some small bombs. Jesus said: *"My people, many terrorists are using other people's lives to make their own political agenda. Your technologies are being abused for evil purposes and inspired by the evil one. The value of life is not even considered by the criminals committing these mass killings. Continue to pray for peace and that these men will be stopped in their deeds of horror."*

I could see an angel going through the clouds of some recent storms. Jesus said: *"My people, I have told you before that you will be seeing worse storms than you have seen before. The power outages are happening more frequently as I warned you as well. Floods, ice storms, and snow will continue to bring havoc to your country. Come to your senses and see that more of you need to be on your knees in prayer. These chastisements continue to test you because of your sins."

I could see the gravesite of our son David. He said: *"I am your little one, David, and I invite you to my grave for a prayer of remembrance. I am in Heaven, but it is important to remember that I am available to help you in your needs. Call on my intercession at any time and I will assist you in prayer. I share my love with all of my parents and Jeanette, Donna and Catherine. Think of me more often than once a year."*

I could see Mary and she was assisting Pope John Paul II. Mary said: *"My dear children, pray for your Vicar of Christ in your Pope John Paul II. He is being tested by those around him and by his health. Your prayers can strengthen him in his daily work. If you do not support him, he will fall easily into the hands of his persecutors. Give him your allegiance and support his teachings even if they be unpopular with your clergy."*

I could see Jesus being immersed in the Jordan as St. John baptized Him. Jesus said: *"My faithful, you need to be Baptized in the Spirit, so you can go forward in your evangelizing efforts. By the power of the Holy Spirit, you will be enriched with the grace to go forward and witness to My Name. Many will try to discourage you from spreading My Gospel, but disregard their taunts. Bringing souls to Me is the most prized gift that you can give Me. Each soul saved causes much rejoicing in Heaven. Even if your efforts are troubled by the evil one, continue to struggle for those souls who may be lost without your help."*

Friday, January 9, 1998:

After Communion, I saw a huge monster with claws trying to kill the light of humanity. Jesus said: *"My people, Satan and his demons are in a desperate hour, and they are trying to snuff out the Faith in the little time that they have remaining. You are besieged by evil on every side as the tribulation is almost upon you. This deluge of rain all around you is an example of how badly your sins need to be cleansed. I have told you of many chastise-*

ments that would strike your land until you would be brought to your knees in prayer. Many have thought nothing will happen, but when you get shaken out of your comfort zone, you will see the need to change your lives. As you are stripped of your possessions, you will see your dependence on My help has always been in front of you. Accept My offer to seek the forgiveness of your sins and you will see following My Will is the best path for your soul."

Later, after Communion, I could see St. Therese in white as a novice and then in brown later. St. Therese said: *"My dear children, I am showing you how much fervor I had to love Jesus when I became a nun. I continued loving Jesus even more until I died. But the faithful should be like this all of their lives as well. Many start out with a deep fervor on their first conversion. It is a brave soul that continues this fervor until their dying day as well. So, I want to encourage all of you to keep close to Jesus in your daily prayer life. Never ease up on your persistence to follow Jesus. The day you try to take it easy, will be the day you let the evil one control you. Every day is a struggle to be with Jesus. So, keep up the good fight every day of your life."*

Saturday, January 10, 1998:

At St. Joseph's Church, Shelton, Conn., I could see some water and there was a reflection of some Roman soldiers. Jesus said: *"My people, you are seeing in this vision a reflection of My time in your own time. Man has not changed that much over the years. There were elite classes in My day as you have them now. Man, today, is still taken up with his pride in doing things for himself. Soldiers are still fighting wars only with better weapons. I came to bring love and peace into the world. But the world rejected Me as much as some reject you for believing in My Name. Even though you have to deal with the fears of man, go out and preach the good news of My love to all men. I came into the world that you may be freed from your sins. Welcome Me into your hearts and you can make a change in the lives of men. Even though man has not changed much over the years, you can add a spiritual dimension to the lives around you. This is in preparation for when all My faithful will live again as Adam. Adam and I were joined as one living in the Divine Will. All of your lives will be* renewed again in My Era of Peace, when you will give Me constant praise as the angels."

Later, at St. Joseph's Church, Shelton, Conn., after Communion, I could see a golden altar and Jesus appeared as He was scourged and placed before Pilate. Jesus said: *"My people, I am showing you Myself as the Lamb of God offered up for your sins. You come for Baptism and I baptize all of My faithful with My blood of saving grace. It is My most precious blood that is poured out over all of you that will save souls and bring you to Heaven. My children, you suffer hardships and disappointments, but do not despair, because I have had to suffer much before you. It is by your suffering that you are purified and made ready to come to Me. I will never leave your side, and I will help you to endure all of your trials. You cannot appreciate a beautiful life of love unless you have struggled. If life was easy all the time, you would never be tested. So, see that your suffering has a grace and it makes you stronger in your faith. Without My help, you cannot survive spiritually. Seek My help every day so you can make your walk up to Calvary. Then I will crown you with a prize of being in love with Me for eternity in Heaven."*

Sunday, January 11, 1998: (Baptism of Jesus)
At St. Joseph's Church, Shelton, Conn., after Communion, I could see Jesus in the tomb. Jesus said: *"My people, if you are My disciples, you must be ready to die if you want to live in Me. You are born to die in this life as a result of Adam's sin. Do not be comfortable with this life, because your time here is very short. You never know when you will be called home to Me in judgment. See that this life is a test of your faith in Me. I am always loving you and I am watching to see your love for Me and your neighbor. Know, My people, that those, who are faithful in this short life, will be raised up in the Resurrection. My Resurrection was My witness of how you will be raised up as well. So, be always prepared in your soul and be willing to serve Me in this life. Your calling comes from your Baptism, since that was the start of your ministry as well as Mine. Be at rest that I will be leading you through life. All I ask is that you follow My commands and you will share in the real life I have planned for you in Heaven."*

Later, at Joe Della Puca's house in Southington, Conn., I could see a church in the winter and I was led out into the hills covered with snow. Jesus said: *"My people, when the schism comes to the churches, you will be forced into the underground church. Those who stay at the schismatic churches will have to discern for themselves when they need to leave. As continuing changes occur in the Mass and when My traditions are violated, there will come a point when their meetings will not have My Presence. Those who go into underground Masses will be in preparation more for the coming Antichrist's power. Those in the schismatic churches will gradually see their churches closed or burned by the Antichrist and his agents. They will not know where to turn, but My remnant will already have been prepared for this religious persecution. My remnant will suffer in the wilderness, but I will protect you from the evil ones. You will share My Eucharistic Presence with My holy remnant priests. It is then that you are to preserve My Host in the monstrance for all to worship. I will not leave you without My Eucharistic Presence until the end of time. I will be faithful in helping you throughout the time of tribulation. Keep your hope and love for Me in your heart before My Sacred Host."*

Monday, January 12, 1998:

At the Immaculate Conception Church, Southington, Conn., after Communion, I could see Jesus turning over the tables in a church. Jesus said: *"My people, you are seeing how the coming schism in My Church is coming about. Many of the churches are more concerned with money and social events than their worship of Me. Some build churches that are void of the saints and only honor the builders instead of Me. They place My tabernacles in places of disrespect. It is almost as if they are embarrassed to have Me present. I ask you, who is more important, you or I? Your churches are to honor and give Me worship. When you honor only man and abort My Masses with your own words, you become an abomination in My sight. When the schism comes and those services no longer call down My Presence, I will close these abominations of desolation, so those sinners will be forced to scatter. My remnant, who will be in underground Masses, I will protect from the evil ones. My faithful, you are the ones who*

will have to preserve My Presence in the True Host. When you can no longer find a proper Mass, you will have to seek Me in Spiritual Communion where I will call My angels to give you My Heavenly Manna. Keep faith in My help even during this trial of the tribulation."

Later, at Frank and Denise Curtin's house Manchester, Conn., I could see the face of Jesus in pain and then His Body on the cross. Jesus said: *"My people, I am showing you how much I love you. I love you with an infinite love. I love you with an unconditional love. I love even those who are condemned in Hell, since I love every creature that I have ever made. This is why I ask you to love even your enemies because it is a perfect love that I ask from you. I died for each of you in the eternal now. That is how I can suffer still for each person's sins. When you commit serious sin, you make Me suffer even more. See, My children, that you cease your sins or I will continue to suffer. Think about each sin as you are committing it as a slap against My face, or another strike from the whip which tears into My flesh. Come, My children, and seek My forgiveness in Confession. Bring your sorrow of your sins to Me and seek My pardon for all the pain that you caused Me by your sins. I will then bestow My grace and peace among you to strengthen you against any further temptation of the evil one. The more you do for Me and the less you sin, the less stripes you will suffer either on earth or in Purgatory. Come rest in My bosom for I long to hold you in My arms forever."*

Tuesday, January 13, 1998:

At Immaculate Conception Church, Southington, Conn., after Communion, I could see a wooden hall as in an old monastery. Jesus said: *"My people, I will be ever faithful to all souls in My love and care for you. Even when you reject Me in sin, My love still reaches out to you. I am your eternal faithful Son of God. I am faithful to My Father and I am faithful to you. These places of holy ground where I have been revered for so long, I will not abandon. I will send My angels to protect these places from all evil demons. These hallowed halls will be your sanctuary even during the tribulation. My holy ground will be honored by My Presence. It is at these places of My safe havens that I will protect you in miraculous ways. I will cure your ills as in the Gospel and I will provide My Heavenly Manna and water. All that you need will be provided. So place your trust in Me at all times and I will guard your souls. Seek Me and My guardian angels will sur-*

Volume X

round you in My protection. Never fear the evil one, only rely on My graces and My love will envelop your souls."

Later, at St. Michael's Ukranian Church, Terryville, Conn., at Adoration, I could see a dove of the Holy Spirit descend on the churches. Many of the modern shapes were falling down. Jesus said: *"My people, you are blessed when you see My traditional churches raised up. Many of the evil people wish to destroy any sense of the sacred. They are more interested in praising man than God. When you raise up those saints, crosses and pictures of Me and My mother, you are restoring the traditions of the Faith that were passed down to you as your heritage from Me. So, preserve all that is sacred, no matter what your peers may criticize. Whatever pleases Me is what you should be doing. It is* the power of My peace that the Holy Spirit brings down among you. This presence in My Spirit is all that you will ever need. Do not be chasing after the peace of man, for it is not long-lasting. My peace is all that you should seek, for if the world all shared in My peace, there would be no evil actions, no wars and no anger. For My peace is based on an infinite love of My heart that I share with all mankind. The sooner you accept My love into your hearts, the more My peace will rest upon you."

At Joe Della Puca's house Southington, Conn., I could see a slim finger of light representing the life of the soul. It then grew dim and finally went out. Jesus said: *"My people, you are seeing the sparks of life darting about in the stubble. These sparks are the souls who have been Baptized into the light of My grace from original sin. During life the souls encounter sin until it becomes so serious, that their spiritual life is snuffed out by mortal sin. I died for you so that you could bring your soul back to Me for the forgiveness of your sins. When you confess your sins, that light of grace is rekindled in your soul. Your life blood is renewed in your spirit and you are spiritually alive once again. Look to the light and condition of your soul at all times, so you can see whether My life burns in you or not. When you are called to judgment, your soul needs to be full of My light. If I come and find your soul dark in death, you will be thrown with the tares into My flaming wrath. Always keep your soul in the light and you will have nothing to fear. You will know your state at all times, since your conscience reveals to you how I see you. When you still have heavy guilt, you know you need to get to Confession. Do not be spiritually lazy, but go and repent so you can remain in My light forever."*

Wednesday, January 14, 1998: (Samuel Reading-Here I am)

After Communion, I could see Jesus on the cross bleeding. Jesus said: *"My son, I have called many messengers to prepare the people over the years. Many of My prophets have had to suffer much, even the giving of their lives for Me in martyrdom. You, My son, may be faced with the same danger. The evil one turns people against My prophets, because they would rather enjoy their sinful pleasures than change their lives. Many of My servants suffer in different ways. Those who suffer pain are act-*

ing on My behalf and they make up for the suffering I would have to endure. My suffering servants endure the pains of others. Give thanks that these souls are making reparation for sins and illnesses. See, My children, that suffering is a part of everyone's life. This suffering, if offered up to Me, can take away some of your time in Purgatory. Do not waste your pain in complaints, but give it up to Me and you will be storing your treasures in Heaven."

Later, at Joe Della Puca's house in Southington, Conn., at a Holy Hour, I could see two large flames on two candles. Then a quick vision of a dove appeared. The Holy Spirit came and said: *"I am the Spirit of Love and I give life to each of your spirits as well. When My Spirit is requested, I bring the Real Presence of Jesus before you. All life is dependent on Me for their being. Every time you see a Consecrated Host, you are experiencing the entire Trinity of Me, the Son and the Father. Give glory and praise to My Spirit for bringing this presence among you. See that when you invoke My help in your speaking, it is I speaking through you, that reveals Jesus to the hearts of those people open to your words. I wish and hope that all men will be drawn to a knowledge of their God and that they will place this grace into action. When you let Me inspire your prayer life, you will be drawn to desire Heaven as your goal."*

Thursday, January 15, 1998:

After Communion, I saw the back of a church and there were several confessionals on either side with penitents in them. Jesus said: *"My people, I am asking you to return to Me in Confession as the loving Father received his prodigal son. My pardon of grace awaits all those who would come to Me in seeking forgiveness of your sins. Do not be afraid to tell your sins to the priest, but think of him as Me waiting to receive you in a loving embrace. Do not listen to the evil one's taunts of how you are unworthy to come to Me. I love even the most grievous of sinners. So, come and receive your Master's joy. Do not be spiritually lazy, but see that cleansing your sins from your soul is a necessity if you are to be saved. Those who remain in their sin and refuse My help are like those without a life preserver in the sinking boat. Come, My chil-*

dren, I welcome all of you into the banquet of forgiveness. All of you are sinners and need My grace of holiness in your souls. Those who have their sins cleansed are like the saints dressed in white robes ready for Me to take them to Heaven."

Later, at the prayer group, I could see lighted little crib scenes in many of the houses. Jesus said: *"My people, as you put away your crib scenes and Christmas decorations, remember to hold My Holy Family in your hearts throughout the year. My love and*

that of My Mother Mary and St. Joseph goes out to you at all times. Let My family unite your own families in love at all times."

I could see some bicycles and thoughts of the Olympic family of nations came. Jesus said: *"My people, as you think about the Olympic games, take your family love one more step into your family of nations. If each family was united with Me in love, your nations would be full of love as well. The more love and peace you can bring into the world, the less chance there will be for wars among nations. The more of My peace that is spread in the world, the closer you will be to My kingdom."*

I could see a prison and the door was opened. Jesus said: *"My people, many times you are made prisoners of your sins. Your earthly pleasures and greed for money have a hold on you which keeps you from loving Me and your neighbor. The grace of the sacraments are the keys to opening your prison and freeing your chains to sin. Come to Me and I will loosen your bonds. Do not let Satan hold you in your distractions, but reach through the bars for your Savior. I give forgiveness to all who seek a pardon. Then you will be released into a new life free from the fetters of the world."*

I could see statues of the saints which were oiling miraculously. Mary said: *"My dear children, share with others your heavenly experience of the bleeding Hosts and the oiling statues. My Son, Jesus, has allowed these manifestations to raise the faith in my children."*

I could see some of the devastation of the ice storms, especially in Canada. Jesus said: *"My people, look on this disaster as a message I have been telling you of how your possessions would be stripped from you. Canada is the country which is trying to implement the Mark of the Beast. This is a lesson what may befall those who worship another god than Me. You are so frail and one touch of My hand throws you into confusion. By helping each other in a common disaster, these neighbors may come to know each other and see the love in helping each other."*

I could see a dark room which had the shades drawn. As the shades were raised, a beautiful sunlit day was shining in. Jesus said: *"My people, do not despair in the darkness of your sin, but open your doors and windows to the light of My Grace. The darkness of*

Prepare for the Great Tribulation and the Era of Peace

Ice Storm in Ottawa, Canada

winter and the cold storms may cause you depression. But lift up your spirits that you have another day to show your love for Me and your neighbor. When you focus on the joy of My love, your happiness will shine out on all those souls around you. When you have happy faces, that will inspire all those who greet you. So, take off your frown faces and turn up the heat of My love in your hearts."

I could see the passenger cars of a train and there was a bright sunlight shining on them. Jesus said: *"My people, this is a sign of the day on which you will be called home to judgment. For those souls that have their lamps ready and their souls cleansed, they will see My light calling them home. Those found wanting without My light will be on another train to perpetuate the darkness that these souls preferred to Me. Stand in My light, all those willing to come to Heaven. You will have to come forward and accept Me, but that leap of faith will gain your Salvation."*

Friday, January 16, 1998:

At St. Ann's Prayer House, Orlando, Florida, I could see Our Lady standing, and under her ran a pipe or drain tile where water was gushing out. Mary said: *"My dear children, you have seen* many times how signs are given to witness heavenly miracles. Just as the grotto in Lourdes was given for healing waters, you will see this again demonstrated to all those who come to the caves for protection in the tribulation. You will call on the Lord and He will cause a spring to come forth to provide you with water to sustain you. Even more miraculously, you will see that this water will provide healing properties for all who are ill and drink of this water. This will be another extension of the mercy of God on all his faithful children. It will also be like the time when Moses provided the water in the desert. Give thanks to God for all He does for you both now and in the trial to come."*

Later, at St. Joseph's Adoration Chapel, Orlando, Florida, I could see the city lights in the buildings at night time. Jesus said: *"My people, you take many of your conveniences for granted until you are without them. When you see the loss of electricity, you feel the effects of this in your bodies. In colder areas you are feeling cold and you are annoyed without your lights or your electrical devices. Yet, when the light of grace in your soul is snuffed out by mortal sin, how many realize that when My grace is gone, you are in deeper peril? My light of grace is much more important than any of your bodily comforts. Yet, how many souls are quick to confess their sins, so My grace can again flow in your souls? The darkness in your soul is much more important and you should be treating it with more care than a return of your earthly lights. See, My children, by touching your comfort zone, I am seeking your trust and your love. If you would be close to Me at all times, you would realize the danger of sin that you place yourselves in during life."*

Saturday, January 17, 1998:

At St. Ann's Prayer House, Orlando, Florida, after Communion, I could see Jesus up above and He was crying tears of love. His tears were falling into the cup on the altar. Jesus said: *"My dear children, you see that I am sobbing tears of love and joy for you at all times. See how My love rains down over you, and it falls in the cup because My consecrated Body and Blood I share with you. I show My love in My tears because it is a heartfelt love which I reach out to all of My souls. You, My children, I am seeking your love in return. It is the agape love of the Spirit which is deep in your soul and your heart. Your tears of love and joy in seeing Me, I treat as precious jewels. To keep your love alive and vibrant, you must keep your communication open to Me. Every prayer you say, it is like saying 'I love you.' to Me. This is why I have likened My love for My Church as in a marriage. Keep My love in your heart by constantly saying how much you love Me. Do not be afraid to express your love for Me in public, but share My love with your brothers and sisters. You are all joined in My One Body, so come share the joy of your Master."*

Sunday, January 18, 1998: (Feast of Cana)

At St. Joseph's Church Orlando, Florida, after Communion, I could see Jesus preaching His Word in a church to a crowd in the pews. Then the people turned to stones and flowers. Jesus said: *"My dear people, I speak out to you all on Sunday through My Gospel. But are you listening intently to My Message? You may hear what is said, but are you putting My Words into your actions? Many come out of duty to Church on Sunday, but you need to live My Message of love throughout the whole week. I tell you, if you do not put My Words into your heart and live your faith, I will raise up these stones and flowers to give Me praise. Listen to what I ask of you. My heart goes out to you and I am crying tears that many have turned away. Come and give Me praise before My*

Blessed Sacrament. Give Me thanks for all the many gifts that I give you and share My love with your neighbors. Help those in need and visit the sick and the imprisoned. When I see you doing these things, I will see your faith in My Words. I love you, My children, and I will reward My faithful in ways you cannot fathom."

Later, at St. Ann's Prayer House Orlando, Florida, I could see a church and there was an opening in the ceiling as a sick person was being let down from the roof to Jesus. Jesus said: *"My people, those who are well do not need a doctor, only sick people do. Come to Me, My children, for I am a doctor of the body and a doctor of the soul. All power resides in Me, so pray to Me for all of your needs. If it be possible, seek My healing power every day and do not wait until your impending death. Even so, I will help those in need of My help, even at the eleventh hour. Those who are sick I will heal in My time, that are not suffering servants. It is the same for penitent sinners that you do not wait until the last moment. Come often for forgiveness, because you know not if you will live to tomorrow. Those who are prayed for may be graced to have a last minute conversion. But do not depend on having that last minute which may never come. Seek My healing power now and continue to bring souls to Me before it is too late for them to be saved."*

Monday, January 19, 1998:

After Communion, I could see a blue sky with a bright light shining down with many rays. Then a flash of a picture with a doorway to Heaven appeared. Jesus said: *"My people, many of you have seen miraculous happenings at places of holiness. These are blessings that I share with My faithful to help them strengthen their faith. Do not look to receive them all of the time, but feel graced if you should experience such miracles. They are also a confirmation of faith experiences. There will be false witnesses and illusions of miracles there also. It is important to discern the spirit of what is occurring. Those who are faithful understand the significance of the doorway to Heaven. I call all of My children to praise and love Me. Those who believe in My blessings will be greatly rewarded."*

Later, at Adoration, I could see an aircraft carrier with its many planes. Jesus said: *"My people, these rumors of war could turn into*

This photograph was taken during John Leary's presentation in Orlando, Florida.

a real conflict that would involve several nations. Many nations are joined in various alliances and this could cause a wider war. The Mid-East area is very tense and one miscalculated move could trigger a major conflict. Because the leaders of the world are so headstrong about their own convictions, pride could start a serious war. With many oil resources at stake, your fuel supplies could again be threatened. Here again, you do not realize all of the effects of a war in this area. Many lives are at stake as well as the oil. Pray, My children, for peace in your world, before it is too late."

Tuesday, January 20, 1998: (Calling of David)
After Communion, I could see in the sky a ring of rulers of the nations. Jesus said: *"My people, your kings and presidents are*

appointed or elected to run your countries. Besides the appointment by men, all of your rulers have to answer to Me, their God. I am the one who watches over their good and bad actions. I read their hearts as they show Me by their deeds whether they are with Me or against Me. They need to have compassion over their people, and not take advantage of their position for their own gain. Those who abuse their office will have to answer to Me in judgment. If they lead the people astray, they may even be subjected to My wrath while in office. Pray for your leaders, because they have heavy responsibilities to lead their people. Your spiritual leaders need even more prayers, since they are responsible for the spiritual welfare of the souls under their care."

Later, at Adoration, I could see a ceiling fan turning. Jesus said: *"My people, the fan turning signifies that the coming events will follow each other in rapid succession. This will be a sign for you of the End Days when you see one disaster after another. This will not be an easy time to endure these hardships. Each storm will continue to strip more people of their possessions. Many will be forced to their knees since their work places will be destroyed. Come, prepare your souls now while you have time."*

Wednesday, January 21, 1998: (St. Agnes, David kills Goliath)
After Communion, I could see a young man — one of God's champions. Jesus said: *"My dear people, many of the prophets and saints were enabled to be successful on the battlefield. Others were willing martyrs to suffer for the sake of My Name. They would rather die than defile their faith. And you, My faithful, how strong will you be when you are put to the test? You realize that these champions of Mine did not achieve their great heights of strength by themselves. It was only through My miraculous help that they were able to achieve these deeds. So it is with you. On your own, you are nothing. It is only by your trust and faith in Me that you will have the courage to defend your faith. Pray to Me for that help every day to give witness to Me. Then when you are drawn into battle with the evil one, you will have My armor of love to defend yourself."*

Thursday, January 22, 1998: (25th ann. Roe-Wade, abortion)

After Communion, I could see a fetus. Jesus said: *"My people, what are you doing in this struggle to stop aborting My babies? Are you speaking out against abortions publicly? Are you helping pregnant women decide for life? In what way are you working to stop this holocaust in your country? Unless you move forward in prayer and deed to stop this evil, it will continue to kill millions of babies. This blood is on the hands of your nation, and by your not voicing an opinion against it, you are passively condoning it. So, fight for your faith and the principles to uphold all rights to life, or your persecution will come sooner. Abortion weighs heavy against your nation. It is for this reason that you are calling down My chastisements against you. If you do not suffer to turn this sin around, you will suffer worse conditions as I strip your possessions."*

Later, at the prayer group, I could see the Infant Jesus and His face was sad. I then could see all of the babies being killed as their souls were rising to Heaven. Jesus said: *"My people, how long will you test My mercy and My justice? You are still killing My babies and without any remorse for your crimes. You have listened to the gods of convenience and luxury instead of bringing your babies to term. Life is more important than any of your excuses for abortion. Struggle to stop this killing or your punishments will increase. You are in an age of apostasy and My faithful need to repent of their sins and keep close to My heart in prayer."*

I could see Pope John Paul II visiting among the poor. Jesus said: *"My pope son, is showing you how to love your neighbor by your works of mercy. Do not be afraid to reach out and help those less fortunate. They need your prayers, your time to help them, and your finances. Remember that you need to give back a part of your wealth to share with the poor. It is your way of thanking Me for watching over you."*

I could see some people who had experienced hardships by floods or a lost job. Jesus said: *"My people, have compassion on those suffering around you. There will be more jobless people being created by corporate cutbacks. Where possible, reach out to your food pantries with help and your donations. Those you help in need are helping My Body as well. Your love and mercy should go out to these unfortunate souls that are being displaced by your rich who are greedy for more profits."*

I could see some grocery stores full of food. Jesus said: *"My people, as long as food is plentiful at your stores, you feel secure and some do not even realize how fortunate you are. It is when you must endure some disasters that your food chain could be placed at risk. I have asked you to store some food for just such events. Do not belittle those saving food, but see the wisdom in being prepared. I will help you in distress, but you must do your part in faith."*

I could see some modern, plain churches. Jesus said: *"My people, you need to put My traditions back in your churches. Your churches are hollow without the feeling of the sacred. Where are My Crucifixes with the Corpus on them? I died for you and you are ashamed to display My remembrance on the cross. How can you know Me if you cannot understand the agony of My suffering for you? See in My cross your own model, so you can follow in My footsteps with your own cross. Keep My Sacred Presence in your church. Without My Presence, it is no longer holy."*

I could see Mary and she was watching over a soup kitchen for the poor. Mary said: *"My dear children, follow the lead of my Son in giving aid to the poor. Wherever you can help them by giving them food, you will be feeding my Son. The homeless need your help, too. Do not feel embarrassed to be among the poor, but reach out to them with your love and mercy as my Son would."*

I could see some small deer with broken legs. Jesus said: *"My people, you reach out to help your animals even with more compassion than those who are handicapped. Reach out to those who have difficulty in wheelchairs or those bedridden, since they are in need of caregivers. Where you can help transport them in their need or bring them food, go forward and help them as if you were helping Me. You need to care for the sick and the handicapped as your works of mercy. When you fail to help your neighbor, these are your sins of omission. Look into their eyes and console all these souls who may be in despair."*

Friday, January 23, 1998: (Pope's visit to Cuba)

After Communion, I could see Pope John Paul II raising the Host at the Consecration of the Mass. Jesus said: *"My people, I am calling My apostles in the readings today, and My pope son, John Paul II is following in the steps of St. Peter. Look to him as your shepherd, for he goes out to all the people of the world bringing My Gospel message of love. Even amidst a communist government in Cuba, he preaches My Word of love to lift up the spirits of the faithful. He is not afraid to speak out about the violation of human rights in Cuba. Look to him as your model in evangelizing souls. Even where you are persecuted, you must preach My Word, so that people all over the world will hear My message and seek conversion of their sins. No matter how grievous the sinner, I call all of My children to Me to share in the mercy of My forgiveness."*

Later, at Adoration, I could see someone holding a magnifying glass and they were on a train. Jesus said: *"My people, this vision indicates a story of how all of the investigations of your president are linked together as in a chain of events. Much of the information and many of the people involved have all disappeared. The information was shredded or burned, while the missing persons have met fatal accidents. Your president is led only by pleasure and fame. He has been a pathological liar in covering up all of his affairs. The startling truth of this man is how far his dictatorial powers have led him without any opposition. The bigger picture is how the One-World People are using him for their own gains. There is no other way such a ruthless man would be allowed to get away with all that he has done. Even if all of the truth would come out on him, it would be stifled by the powers behind the scenes. Only when the One-World People are through using him, will he be exposed. Until then, the media will protect him. The bottom line of this evil is that all of these evil people will answer to Me soon, as I will conquer all of their plans. They will then see that their lies, killings and subterfuge will be laid bare, and they will pay for their crimes with My justice."*

Saturday, January 24, 1998:

After Communion, I could see some teeth and it meant someone lying while they were smiling. Jesus said: *"My people, the sin of pride many times is at the root of other sins. In order to save face and avoid revealing your faults, many resort to lying* about themselves. What is evil about this habit is that it perpetuates itself into a lifestyle of not telling the truth. It is better to admit to yourself that you are not perfect rather than be living a lie about your life. It becomes an even worse situation when you start affecting other lives by forcing them not to reveal truths about your misdeeds. So, stop your lying in the first place and you never have to make excuses for yourself again. Remember that the truth will set you free, but lying will make you a prisoner of your own sins."

Later, at Adoration, I could see some praying hands and then hands reaching out for mercy. Jesus said: *"My people, many of you have good intentions to say your prayers and seek My mercy in forgiveness. You may have special social events which may prevent you from following through on your intentions. Other days you may fall asleep before you can finish your prayers. But, if you generally keep your word and say your prayers when you have time, I will understand your good intentions and credit you for your intentions. I know if you do not waste your time and are faithful to Me that you would carry out your plans. Know that I am a forgiving and merciful God. I will count your blessings even at times when you cannot fulfill all of your commitments."*

Sunday, January 25, 1998:

After Communion, I could see a wooden circular ceiling in a church or synagogue. Jesus said: *"My people, today's reading speaks of My fulfillment of Scripture at My First Coming. What you are reading now is the beginning of the fulfillment of the End Days. All that is in the Bible has to take place, because it is the Word of God. So, have your souls ready as the wise virgins, for these events have been placed into motion. All that is necessary technologically is in place. The time of the Antichrist is about to begin, but do not question the dates. It will happen in My time, when I see fit and no sooner. It is a grace to be forewarned of these events, and My warning may be needed by some to wake them out of their complacency. My love will always be present among you. Do not get comfortable with your worldly ways, for when these events occur, your faith will be tested to the limit of your endurance."*

Later, at Adoration, I could see flags of different nations on a war table. Jesus said: *"My people, look through the smoke screen of the latest testing of your president by the One-World People. They are attempting to take more power away from you by fiat orders. While the press bombards you with allegations, the world scene will take advantage of your seeming weakness. Iraq will continue to take liberties, further endangering a miscalculated war. Just as your country and Canada have been tested by blackouts, think of what would happen if your gasoline was endangered. Many events will be occurring so fast that you will not know what will hit you from the blind side next. Be spiritually prepared by frequent Confession and your daily prayers and you will be able to stand up to the attacks of the Antichrist."*

Monday, January 26, 1998:

After Communion, I could see the silhouette of someone talking in the dark. Jesus said: *"My people, the tongue of gossip can be very vicious in destroying a person's reputation. If it be by malicious slander, it is even a worse sin where what was said was untrue. But even if what is said is true, it is still damaging without that person there to defend themselves. So, My friends, curb your tongue when what you say may ruin someone's reputation. Even if that person is not found out publicly, I see all and I will judge that person. It is not for you to judge, but only to advise your brother or sister of their wrongdoing. Do not worry that someone will not be brought to justice, since in the end all of you must make an accounting of your deeds before Me. Those judged will then have to pay for their crimes wherever they are sent."*

Later, at Adoration, I could see a snake dangling in the forest. Jesus said: *"My people, beware of the evil one, Satan, the fallen Lucifer. Let his falling from grace be an example to you that anyone can fall, no matter how holy they may be. You need to be vigilant of the evil one around you who is always lurking to steal souls away from Me. Do not be fooled by those that say that there is no personal devil. He is an evil being and he does exist. Be ever watchful, for he will tempt you when you are most weak, from sleep, or even when you relax your prayers. Your weapons are prayer and your guardian angel. Know also that he will tempt you most with your most frequent sins. Be ready for his attacks and you can better stifle your weakness to these sins. If a man is ready for the thief, his house will be protected. But if you grow lazy and let down your spiritual guard, the evil one will strike when you least suspect him. So, be ever on guard, for you will be tempted to your dying day. The more you build up your spiritual life with daily prayer, Holy Communion, Confession, fasting and adoration, the more armor you will have to fight off this wretch. Know that I and your angel are at your side. Call on My Name whenever you need to rid the evil one."*

Tuesday, January 27, 1998:

After Communion, I could see some yellow flowers and a sense of joy in the Lord. Jesus said: *"My people, when you have Me truly Present in Holy Communion, there is reason to be joyful that your Lord greets you. Again, you are grateful that I come among you as a great healer of all of your sicknesses and your down emotions. I lift you up with a love that has no comparison, since it is the love of your creator that I share with you. You have comfort in My Presence, since I love the sinner just as much as one who did not sin. Place your trust and faith in My grace that I will protect you from the evil one. Just call on My Name, and I will be at your side. Do not forget to ask My help every day when you consecrate your day to Me. Know that My love is overwhelming and reach out to show your love for Me. By your prayers of petition and thanks, I will honor your intentions in your love for Me."*

Later, at Adoration, I could see some circular caves as a place of protection. Jesus said: *"My people, places underground may afford you the best protection for the End Days to come. Should any wars reach a nuclear dimension, you would be safer from bomb damage and the radioactive fallout in a cave. Man seems to be running to this Battle of Armageddon with reckless abandon. Your leaders talk of war, but they do not see all the problems in containing an outbreak with possibly many nations. I tell you to think carefully before entering into a war that you may not be able to stop. With so many nations having nuclear weapons, it will be just a matter of time until they are used. Pray for peace like you have never prayed before. If the anger among nations is* not compromised, you will see a wasteland on the earth that nature may not be able to change. It will be My renewal of the earth that will bring things back in order, such that man will never again despoil it."*

Wednesday, January 28, 1998:
After Communion, I could see a deep bunker in the ground and then a map of Iraq. Jesus said: *"My people of America, do not let your pride or your military leaders talk you into a war in Iraq. Your purposes in bringing war there are not truly defending any of your interests. This is only a means to give warning for a protection of your oil companies' interests which in turn fuels the One-World People. This war could only split your nations and cause further anger among the Arab countries. When you stop battling for the One-World Order, you will frustrate their One-World control. Pray to stop this potential war or you will live to regret it."*

Thursday, January 29, 1998:
After Communion, I could see someone go into their favorite pew at church. Jesus said: *"My people, you truly are creatures of habit and you go to places that you are the most comfortable. Look at life as many decisions that you have to make each day. Many become how they appear by what they choose to eat. Your work is a result of how much effort you wish to put into your education. You choose where you wish to live and what vocation you want in life. Many of these decisions have to be made, but one decision that you make over and over is how you will respond to My love. A tree is known by its fruit. So it is with you. If you love Me and your neighbor, you will bear a fruit of good works to help each other. If you dislike Me or ignore Me, you will be selfish and not help others. You are who you are by your decisions each day. So, make your decisions based on following My Divine Will and you will be choosing Heaven over eternal pain in Hell."*

Later, at the prayer group, I could see warplanes, submarines, warships and bombs falling. Jesus said: *"My people, do not play this game of brinkmanship where one nation dares another to strike. Many lives are at stake in the Middle-East and it should not* be a trivial decision to try and punish Sadam for seeking food for his people. The evil one is busy at work trying to get a war started. Pray, My people, that you can compromise your differences. War is not a decision, it is a vote for destruction with no winners."

I could see some businesses closing their doors and others out of work from layoffs. Jesus said: *"My people, even though your economy is doing well, still the rich are demanding more profits. If your jobs are cut too much, you may see a self-inflicted recession strike your land. The rich in the stock market will see that it was the people who generated the wealth and not the corporations. All of this will come down on you because of your greed for money."*

I could see some people in wheelchairs being cared for. Jesus said: *"My people, you need to go the extra mile in helping those who need your help. Do not be selfish with your time, but reach out and help your neighbor as if you were helping Me. When love develops in your heart, you will be willing to share your time and money with others. It is those who are selfish that will be cold and lacking in love."*

I could see a soup kitchen where they were feeding the poor. Jesus said: *"My people, I have been making a point of helping the poor with the basics in life, because it is everyone's responsibility, not just a few. If you cannot help in food distribution, do what you can to give these organizations your financial help. The poor you always have with you, but you cannot forget to give them a hand in their survival."*

I could see a night scene with only a few lights, then a day time picture of swollen rivers. Jesus said: *"My people, all over your country you are experiencing trials from rain, snow and ice. See in these chastisements a message that is going on deaf ears. I have forewarned you that unless your sins of abortion and your sins of the flesh are not curbed, you will continue to witness one major event after another. Continue your prayers to reverse these sins, before My justice will exact your punishments."*

I could see some walls lit by the sunlight and it gradually darkened for awhile from an eclipse of the sun. Jesus said: *"My people, this sign in the skies, that you will be seeing shortly by the coming eclipse, will be a sign of dramatic events about to take place. The darkness of evil is spreading over your land and there are not enough praying to offset the evil around you. The scales of My justice show My cup is overflowing with the need for retribution due to your sins. How long do you expect Me to hold back My hand, when you worship your earthly gods more than Me? Change your lives by giving Me glory and praise or all of your gods will be brought down around your feet."*

I could see some locks on hearts and some wallets. Jesus said: *"My people, I have not seen such a self-indulgent society as the one you have. You have become a people seeking instant gratification in every worldly desire that you have. If you cannot have something now, you are frustrated into despair that you cannot be satisfied. Why are you spending so much of your time seeking after the worldly goods, when you should be seeking Heavenly treasures first? Work harder on your salvation, for that will last forever. Do not waste so much time on the earthly things that will be thrown in the wastebin tomorrow."*

Friday, January 30, 1998:

After Communion, I could see a great ball of fire like the sun and it was spinning and white sparks were flying out from it. Jesus said: *"My people, I have given you many messages to watch for the signs in the sky as the End Days approach. This sign of the spinning sun you have witnessed yourself at places of apparition. These are given as a physical evidence to buoy your faith. But do not rely entirely on such signs, because you must test the spirit of every message given. I have shown you these sparks that will be seen in the skies to give you a sign of the coming events on the earth. You have asked for a testing of this message and it is truly from Me as you have witnessed by many confirmations of what was given earlier. I tell you, My people, be on guard because My adversary will try to deceive you with his own signs and wonders, which the Antichrist will be allowed to perform. If someone comes and claims to be Me, do not believe them. Only when I come on the clouds in great glory and the evil ones flee before Me, are you to believe that it is My Second Coming. Satan will not fight himself in the Antichrist, but these evil men and evil spirits will openly ask Me to leave because their time has come."*

Later, at Adoration, I could see a missile traveling through the clouds. Then, I saw some mushroom clouds of nuclear bombs going off. Jesus said: *"My people, you are on the brink of some serious decisions. If you do not show signs of strength, Sadam will continue to thwart your inspections. But if you threaten the use of force, you may have to carry it out. Any decisions favoring war will have to be very measured or other nations may come to support Iraq against you. It is this added dimension of not knowing the reaction of other nations that may trigger a miscalculated war. Your best move is to not make threats that you are not willing to carry out. All of these war rumors could cause a lot more trouble than any financial crisis. Live in peace with one another, since the war option will not solve any problems."*

Saturday, January 31, 1998:
After Communion, I could see a gold cup filling up with wine. Jesus said: *"My people, your sins cause Me to suffer in atonement for your offenses. You are the one who must come forward to receive My forgiveness. Seek Me in contrition for your sins and I will forgive you. For I am always merciful in forgiving your sins. Do not feel unworthy, but come to Me and I will refresh your soul. Your sins that I have forgiven are far from Me, but still you must suffer the temporal punishment due for your sins. My justice calls for retribution when you break My commands. You remember how Adam and Eve were banished from the Garden in punishment of their sin. As a result, all men are now weak to sin and you need your souls to be refreshed by My grace. See that you are sinners and need frequent Confession to stay in sanctifying grace. All of your suffering both here and in Purgatory will be applied against this temporal punishment you must pay. Stay close to Me in My sacraments and you will always be safe."*

Later, at St. Michael's Church in Oreb, Ohio, I could see a mountain before me against a blue sky. Jesus said: *"My people, your joy will reach fever pitch when you have Me wholly in your heart. The vision of the mountain shows you a message of hope that I have left with all of My disciples. I took three of My apostles up Mt. Tabor so that I could be transformed before their eyes. They saw Me in a radiant body that all of you will share in the Era of Peace.*

See that My Transfiguration was a sign of the mystery of the Trinity, and it was a promise of a new life for all who believe in Me. This is the mountaintop experience that many talk of and which all of My people will share. Rejoice, My faithful, for My dazzlingly white radiance I will share with you at My Second Coming. Then, evil will be removed and you will live a holy life in My Divine Will. This is the hope that I give to all of those who suffer now in persecution so you will one day share in My glory. Pray for perseverence in faith and your reward will be eternal life with Me."

Sunday, February 1, 1998:

At St. George's Church, Georgetown, Ohio, after Communion, I could see an altar made out of marble and later a bridge. Jesus said: *"My people, I am showing you this altar so that you realize it is truly My Body and Blood that is being sacrificed at every Mass for your sins. In the Old Testament you have seen how blood offerings were made on altars in giving them up to God. I am the pure unblemished Lamb being offered up for the forgiveness of your sins. See in this act of My giving of My life, a perfection in My love for all of mankind. It is your most important decision in your life to realize that in fact you are sinners and are in need of My healing graces. Without the sorrow for your sins and that seeking to have them forgiven, how can you partake of My offering of salvation? You need to love Me and accept Me as your Savior and Lord of your life. All My love is given to you. I await your loving response to Me for all that I have given you. Come walk in My love and grace so I can show you the way to your salvation. When you pick up your cross and carry it to Calvary, you are imitating the suffering I had to go through. When you follow My commands and are led by My Divine Will, you will see the glory of your resurrection in sharing eternity with Me. Come to Me, My people, and share in My love and My rest."*

Later, at Adoration, I could see some beautiful glass doors inside a building and then some massive destruction with debris all over as with a tornado or an earthquake. Jesus said: *"My people, you think that you have everything under control, but a day is coming when your affluent peace will turn into sudden destruction. Plans are being made now to take over the world under the excuse of a world war. The One-World People will allow this destruction, so when the pieces are picked up, the Antichrist will then take over as a man of peace. Do not be deceived by these false wars or the Antichrist's empty promises. Believe only in My Word where truth will reign supreme. Take My love into your heart and do not be concerned about money and possessions."*

Monday, February 2, 1998: (Feast of the Presentation)
I could see some metal brackets coming together in a perfect fit. Jesus said: *"My people, I am the Master Builder, the Creator of all that is in the universe. This vision of things fitting perfectly*

is how I craft all that you see both on earth and in the heavens. Every object, person or animal has come from My willing it so and even its continued existence. I have given man and the angels free will that you can come to a love of Me on your own. Much like I have planned all of creation, I have a plan for each of your lives. It is your free will choice to discover who you are and how you fit into My Master Plan. Everything that happened to Me on earth was planned as well. All of My plans have been revealed to you by prophecy and all of them had to be fulfilled in My time on earth. So it is with the present age. My prophecy in revelation is still being fulfilled as the End Days will soon bring an end to this era of evil. Once I have removed the evil ones and all the consequences of Adam's sin, you will see a new earth, and man following more in My Divine Plan according to My Divine Will. Without evil, you will see how I originally planned man's existence much like the angels to know, love, and serve Me."*

Later, at Adoration, I could see Mary and Jesus standing together. Mary said: *"My dear children, I wish to share with you that Simeon's prophecy was the story of my sorrows throughout my Son's life. I gave you those words of 'do whatever He tells you' because my heart and soul are always one with Jesus. As He suffered in His bodily torments, I suffered those same pains in my heart. All of you, my children, are suffering your own torments in this life. Some are called to suffer in the body, while others are to share their pain in the heart. Offer up all of your pain and your struggles to Jesus as you walk with Him bearing your own cross to Calvary. When you unite yourselves in His One Mystical Body, your pain is shared with Jesus and He lifts you up to bear all you are given. See, my children, that despite all of your trials, you are to keep your faith and hope focused on Jesus. One day you will live and share in His glory for all you had to suffer on this earth. My child, I am affirming again that you will not see me much longer."*

Tuesday, February 3, 1998: (St. Blaise)

After Communion, I could see some people at Mass and then another scene of shrubs in a broad landscape. Jesus said: *"My people, just as the woman today in the Gospel reached out to touch Me for a healing, many are still reaching out to Me with the same faith. In addition to physical healings, there are many in need of psychological or spiritual healings as well. Come to Me, My friends, for I am the great healer of all mankind's problems. Many forget to reach out and ask for My healing graces, but I am always there for those who seek them in faith. As with many of the healings that I performed, your soul needs to be cleansed of its sin before the rest of the body can be healed. The healing grace of the soul can than go out to invigorate the body as well. So, when you pray for healings, do what you can to get that sick person to Confession first. Many of your illnesses can stem from guilt feelings that need to be addressed before the body can be healed. Even for the impossible cases, you need to come to Me in faith. I will listen to all of your prayers and answer them according to My Will which is best for your souls."*

(Mass for Joseph Trunfio) At Joseph Trunfio's house after Communion, I could see some people at their home getting ready for dinner. Jesus said: *"My people, do not wait until imminent death to realize how precious life is to you. You are all appointed a given time without knowing when you will die. Remember that you are a spiritual being made to My image, to know, love, and serve Me. You have a blend of a spiritual body in an earthly body. Look on each life as special with a part of Me in them. Even the unborn have a right to life as much as any one of you. Do not pick and choose which life is more valuable, but know that each life is equal before Me. Treasure this gift of life that each of you shares with each other. You all are on loan to each other for a time. So look on each life as a special gift for you to experience. Love one another and love Me as well. For all of My creation was created out of love. This is why I have placed new life in the love of the marriage bond and do not defile it. The more you share in My Divine Love, the more you will be led to follow Me on your road to Heaven. Go now and show your love for all of mankind, while you have the opportunity to share with them."*

Wednesday, February 4, 1998:

After Communion, I could see someone in white robes from the waist down walking around the pews in a church. Jesus said: *"My people, I want to stress endurance of the faith in your fast-paced society. Many of the people in your society are open to hear about miracles or unusual messages from various visionaries. You look on most things as a fast-paced news story for the day and then move on to the next story. Even if I were to walk among you for one day, your faith may be raised, but would this spirit last? You all have itching ears for the next message, but are you truly learning from them to make a difference in your life? Enough messages have been given to you to more than save your society, but you give a deaf ear by your actions the next day. Many of the people are like the seed which fell on the rocks or among the thorns. You have little root in faith and wither, or you let the pleasures of life distract you from the fervor of your first conversion. Do not just give Me lip service. You must take My message of love and live it in all you do. When you help your neighbor with acts of kindness, and worship Me everyday, then you will be on the right road to Heaven. You need to be long-standing in your faith to survive the temptations and trials of this life. Take heed from My messengers by letting the Gospel message become a part of your life."*

Thursday, February 5, 1998:

After Communion, I could see a bonfire with many people around it warming themselves. Jesus said: *"My people, I am showing you how a little war, once started, can ignite into a larger war. Why are your leaders threatening war, even in the face of other leaders of opposition suggesting a world war could result? Look into why your leaders are demanding air strikes, even when they admit it would not solve the problem. Listen to My earlier advice and do not start something that you cannot finish. Your interests in a foreign land on suspicions do not warrant such a gamble on starting a world war. Continue, My people, in your prayers for peace and pray also that your leaders will come to their senses in this potential disaster. It is no time to be testing your new weapons and satisfying your pride at the expense of many innocent lives. Stop this reckless charge to kill as well as your reckless killing of the unborn."*

Later, at the prayer group, I could see Mary coming as Our Lady of Fatima. Mary said: *"My dear children, I have stopped* giving public messages to many of my messengers. This is a sign to you that you will soon see all of my messages stop. Again, as events become more frequent, you will be fulfilling many of the secrets given out at my places of apparition. You all need to be in preparation, for these events will soon be occurring. Pray often for peace and all the trials coming so you are able to endure them."

I could see some army officers and many pictures were being taken of them. Jesus said: *"My people, why do you pride yourself in your many weapons and armies. You underestimate the potential in this current Middle-East compromise. I am telling you in every way possible to stop this madness of your leaders. Satan is stirring up these war clouds so he can cause the strife and chaos that will usher in the Antichrist."*

I could see a vision of the College of Cardinals electing a new pope. Jesus said: *"My people, this Pope of Mine, you have now, you need to cherish and protect. He is My last faithful Pope before the Antichrist and the Antipope dominate the scene. They will bring up charges and criticisms of John Paul II so they can elect this evil pope, who will reign next. Pray much for John Paul II for he will be leading My remnant church."*

I could see a green train that was being used to carry prisoners to the detention centers. Jesus said: *"My people, your time of persecution draws closer. Believe what I have been telling you in preparing some food, and getting ready to leave for the rural areas. Call on Me and My angels and they will lead you to places of protection. You will see some martyred for My Name, but take heart that they will be safe with Me. Your strength will be tested. Do not be concerned about money and your possessions, for they will fall by the wayside."*

I could see some children and some large crowds. Jesus said: *"My son, you need to go quickly among My people and teach them of the coming End Times. Many are foolishly discarding My Words of preparation and cannot believe that their judgment time comes near. Pray much, My children, for My End Times lie at the door. Believe in the signs foretold in the Scriptures, because you are now witness to them."*

I could see some chairs falling over and it was a sign of some of your leaders being overthrown. Jesus said: *"My people, do not think that your governments will be stable much longer. All of your nations will be tested by wars and famines as the pestilence will soon visit your people. Already you are being tested by rain storms and other disasters. How can you deny that these events are a sign of the End Days? You must focus more on prayer and My protection, for this is all that will get you through this time."*

I could see some old white stones in a cemetery and some new stones as well. Jesus said: *"My people, by your actions you hold your fate in your own hands. Choose life, My children, and not death in wars and abortions. It is your actions that you will be held accountable for. How will you answer to Me if you stood idly by, not struggling for peace or to stop your abortions? Work now against these evils before they consume you. You do not have much longer to voice your choice for life, so go quickly in what you must do."*

Friday, February 6, 1998:

After Communion, I could see some people being tortured and put to death in the early days of Christianity. Jesus said: *"My people, look at the arrogance of power in Herod when he had St. John the Baptist beheaded. Because of his own desire and pride, he thought nothing of killing to save face among his peers. This arrogance of power and killing for convenience has been a curse among rulers of your world down through the ages, even until today. Because your leaders have little regard for how precious life is, they kill at random whenever it suits their purpose. This mentality against life is being felt throughout your whole society, as your mothers are now your new executioners killing their own babies. Do not think that those who kill will get off free. My mercy will forgive those sorrowful for their sins, but all killers will have a huge price to pay on their judgment. They will either pay on earth, in Purgatory or in the ravages of Hell, but they will not escape My wrath of justice. Pray, My people, that you seek the forgiveness of your sins, for those sinners, who do not repent, will suffer an eternity of pain in Hell."*

Later, at Adoration, I could look out the bore at the breach of an artillery gun. Jesus said: *"My people, I am showing you what might result from your involvement with a war in Iraq. If you become embroiled in a major war, your troops would be stretched thin to bring them overseas. This thin pretext for a war is a fabrication so you would have less troops at home. This would leave you open for a planned takeover which could come at any time. Do not be surprised one day when you will be occupied by United Nations foreign troops under the guise of security or environmental protection. Your days of freedom are not much longer. Look into history and you will see how I allowed My own people to be scattered because of their offenses against Me. You will experience the same loss of your freedom in payment for all of your sins of abortion and your sins of the flesh. Then your chastisements of the weather will be mild compared to the abuse that you will soon suffer at the hands of the Antichrist and the One-World People. Pray, My children, for soon your comforts will be taken away and you will be prisoners in your own land. When you are brought to your knees in submission, you will seek My help to relieve you of your oppression."*

Saturday, February 7, 1998:

At St. Dominic's Church, Springfield, Kentucky after Communion I could see a church altar and St. Therese came and stood before me dressed as a Carmelite. St. Therese said: *"My dear child, I come to support you in your work of evangelization. You know how much I love Jesus. I lived, breathed, and shared with my Jesus in my heart. I am fulfilled to be with Him now. Your work is very important and there is a great need for the people to be led back to God. Continue to encourage the people you meet to practice their faith in all that they do. When you make the Gospel a part of your life, you are walking with Jesus. I ask you also when you are praying to invoke the names of the saints, especially those of us you know very well. Seek our help in guiding you by calling out our names. We are more than willing to seek intercession for you with Jesus. Pray my little way each day and seek to do the will of Jesus in all that He asks of you."*

Later, at St. Dominic's Church, Springfield, Kentucky, after Communion, I could see some large triangles with smaller triangles in the middle. In the center triangle I could see Satan imprisoned and suppressed. Jesus said: *"My people, to know the Trinity of*

God the Father, God the Son, and God the Holy Spirit is a mystery of your faith. Yet, all power resides in God over everything that happens. I am showing you that the Devil's power is nothing before Me. I only allow these temptations, but I never let him test you beyond the grace that I give you to overcome the devil. Whenever you are tested, call on My Name and the Devil will be dispatched. Do not give credit to the evil one for more than he is allowed to accomplish. In the end you are to blame for your sins. All those who are condemned to Hell are there because they refused My grace and love and allowed themselves to indulge in behavior against My laws. Get hold of yourself and choose to follow My Will before it is too late and you lose yourself to Satan. Do not blame anyone else for your sins, since you are the victim of your own decisions. You cannot be saved on your own. Come to Me and I will lead you to your salvation, but you must give your will over to follow Me."

Sunday, February 8, 1998:

At St. Dominic's Church, Springfield, Kentucky, after Communion, I could see a soldier dressed in gold in front of the altar. Jesus said: *"My people, I am preparing My army of faithful to go before Me to evangelize the people with the Word of the Gospel. You need to put on the breastplate of faith and the armor of trust in Me. As you walk with your guardian angels into the battle, I will support you in leading souls to Me. You are in a battle of good and evil and you will face principalities and powers. Do not be fearful of the evil forces against you, but have trust that My power will overcome the evil ones. Even though you may struggle for souls, fight the good fight and never let down your guard against the evil one. It is when you are blessed in the Spirit that you will be protected from all harm. Pray daily that your strength will carry you into the battle with the Word of God at your side."*

Later, at Alice Blozina's house, Marion, Kentucky, after Communion, I could see Jesus on a small crucifix and there was a small Mass kit on the table. (We had just picked up our new Mass kit.) Jesus said: *"My dear remnant, today you are sharing a home Mass which may soon become the way of the underground Masses. A time is coming when a schism will spread throughout My Church.*

My faithful remnant will be led by Pope John Paul II, as you will be tested to decide between the Antipope's side and those who will defend My Name. A false pope will be elected and he will mislead many to follow the Antichrist. This schismatic church will take control of your churches. The priest and laity will then have to choose between Me or the Antichrist. You will be fortunate to find an underground Mass. Fear not, My people, for if you cannot have a Mass, you can seek Me in a Spiritual Communion. I will then send My angels among you to feed you My Heavenly Manna. By My Real Presence I will continue to be

among you even to the end of time. Have faith in My protection and I will grant you all of your hearts's desire in Me."

Monday, February 9, 1998:
After Communion, I could see a reflection in a pond of a window from a Gothic Church. Jesus said: *"My people, you are seeing in this vision that My Church is a reflection of Me. I came to the earth as the victim soul of all time to die for you and redeem your souls. You reflect Me in that you are made to My image and likeness. When you look at all of those in My Church, you are looking at My Mystical Body. I have given you a miraculous gift in My Sacrament of Holy Communion, since I share My Real Presence with you every day. Many of My faithful realize the grace of My gift and attend daily Mass and Communion. This daily giving of Myself to you in the sacrifice of the Mass, allows you to have that Divine Union with My Spirit every day. Treasure the Mass as a special gem of My love, for it will soon be taken away from you. As the evil one will have his hour, many of your blessings will be stripped from you, and you will be tested in your faith to see how much you love Me under persecution."*

Later, I could see some dark colored birds picking at a dead animal. (Today, we saw crows on the road picking at a dead carcass.) Jesus said: *"My people, this is the vision of the scavenger birds returning to Israel. When the War of Armageddon comes, these will be the same birds that will pick the flesh from the dead bodies at war. This is an ominous sign of the End Days, but it is a stark reminder to you what a world war could lead to. I continue to warn you, My friends, that this confrontation that your leaders are contemplating is being designed by the evil one in concert with the One-World People. This is a war that has no real basis for starting, but it may lead into a much wider war if other nations get involved. Back away from this unclear objective and strive for peace instead of testing Saddam with a war that only a few are controlling. Pray for peace or you could face World War III."*

Tuesday, February 10, 1998:
After Communion, I could see some beautiful metal pieces being fire polished. Jesus said: *"My people, in this vision I am con-*

stantly refining you like silver. You are like a piece of metal coming out of the mold that needs the rough edges refined. My faithful have accepted My yoke upon their shoulders, but now they must be tried in the fire of My love. No longer do you follow your ways or man's ways, now you must do everything imitating My Plan for you. When you follow your Master as your leader, you are aspiring to reach holiness in following My commands. But you are not a slave to just follow Me, you are following out of love and I am only gently showing you a way to your salvation. All of those who accept My way instead of man's traditions are understanding the need to be perfected on their way to Heaven. You need to have the proper wedding garment before you can join My banquet. Purify your sins in Confession and come follow Me in My work."

Later, at Adoration, I could see a very large gong being struck. Jesus said: *"My people, this sounding of the gong is a sign to you that the time of the great tribulation is about to begin. It is so close that you can almost sense its coming. All the signs of this time are already evident. Events of your weather and the rumors of war are all converging to the time when the Antichrist will be announced. You will see events falling one right after the other and if war breaks out, it could move faster. Once the world chaos reaches fever pitch, it will be the time for the evil one's entrance to his public declaration. You will need much prayer and fasting to endure this trial. Prepare, My people, for your trial is about to begin."*

Wednesday, February 11, 1998:

After Communion, I could see a movie theater and it was empty. Jesus said: *"My people, your movies have been so corrupted that they are empty of any morality. Because you have been exposed to so much violence and perversion, each new movie tries to outdo the last one. These movies are a testimony on how much your society has allowed. Promiscuity and the like have been encouraged since the morals of your society are at a low ebb. You see children abused and many killings in the street over drugs. Many of these suggestions of hate and lust are evidenced in your movies. In order to clean up your society, give example to others of your distaste of these evils by not attending your movies. Your TV programming is another area to shun your viewing. Unless your young people have good example, they will fall victims of the immorality of your entertainment. Your best complaint is to avoid all contact with this contagion of sin."*

At Joseph Trunfio's house, I could see Mary come to Bernadette of Lourdes in the darkness with a bright light shining on each of them. Mary said: *"My dear children, there is a great need for healing in many cases of the sick all over the world. It is most important that the souls of the sick be healed spiritually first. The spiritual healings are most powerful. Pray that those who are sick be blessed with my Son's grace to have their sins forgiven in Confession. Healings of the body need strong faith and that it be in the will of my Son, Jesus. Many souls are suffering servants for the sins of the world. Offer up all of your prayers and sufferings for those sinners who have no one to pray for them. The witness of those accepting their pain is an inspiration to all of you. You all need to share with each other to comfort those in pain and their loved ones. You are all a part of my Son's Mystical Body, and when one part hurts, all the members share in that pain with Jesus. Pray for all of those hurting with illness and visit them whenever you can."*

Thursday, February 12, 1998:

After Communion, I could see some shiny new metal parts of missiles sitting on train tracks in a cave. Jesus said: *"My people, you are sitting on the edge of a major war about to explode with devastating results. I am showing you many weapons which Saddam has hidden away in the hills. If these and other weapons are brought into the battle, many people would be at risk from these weapons of mass destruction. By your worship of science in making deadlier weapons over time, you have created all of the means for a world war that could threaten all life on earth. You have abused all of the things of the earth to make yourselves comfortable, but with evil intents in destroying your enemies. You see the hand of the evil one in stirring up this war, since he wants man to destroy himself. Pray, My children, for if these weapons are unleashed, your very lives will be threatened all over the earth. Your destructive intentions will be neutralized when I intervene in your events. Before you destroy yourselves, I will inactivate all of your weapons. My chastisements will bring Satan and his plans to an end as My Triumph will conquer him before he can carry out his destruction of man."*

Later, at the prayer group, I could see many leaders circled at a table in the UN. Then Mary came with her Rosary. Mary said: *"My dear children, I thank you for your many Rosaries tonight. I call on you to pray sincerely for peace in the Middle-East. Every day make an extra effort to say your fifteen decades for peace in the world. Many of your leaders are speaking war cries instead of a true spirit of compromise. Stop this war before it starts. The risks never outweigh the lives and the destruction that war brings. Live in peace or your wars will affect your own peace no matter where you live."*

I could see a hangman's stand with the noose. Jesus said: *"My people, many of your states are bringing back capital punishment. This is being played up in your media to show how cruel you have become in your punishment. Part of this publicity could be to get you used to frequent killing so when the persecution comes, martyrs will be common place. Once you have a low value for life, killing becomes more acceptable. Your death culture is being readied for the tribulation."*

I could see a globe of the earth and it was clouding up with more clouds. Jesus said: *"My people, the ocean currents continue to generate more storms of destruction. All that you have done to your environment is coming back to punish you for your abuses. The fury of these storms is a continuing chastisement for your many sins. I forgive you, but the elements of nature must carry out its course. You have set these warming trends in motion, so now you must pay the consequences."*

I could see a new wasteland as a result of fires and severe storms. Jesus said: *"My people, many are seeing their homes destroyed by earthquakes, fires and tornadoes. Water and natural disasters are happening with more frequency. I told you that events would quicken and you are seeing this fulfilled. Soon many will be stripped of their comforts and they will see how fragile their lives are. Make amends for your sins or your debts will drag you down deeper in disaster."*

I could see some older people talking. Jesus said: *"My people, you have little respect for the wisdom of those who have experi-*

enced life. Many of your cultural traditions have been lost. It is this passing down of a good morality that is necessary for a society to treasure a proper lifestyle. With freedoms and rights blinding your wisdom, you have discarded all respect for My Commandments. When a society turns a deaf ear to Me, you are doomed to repeat the demise of previous civilizations. Protect your families from this evil decay and bring prayer and spiritual order into your society or you will collapse under your own sins."

I could see some gears being made in a factory. Jesus said: *"My people, your factories are going to grind to a halt when you can no longer find a market for your products. As incomes go lower and foreign labor drives wages down, there will be fewer buyers. Your factory labor is continuing to disappear. I have told you that you will return to a rural life because your living standard will drop. This displacement of work will cause financial hardships. This again is how your things will be taken away from you as your blessings cease because of your sins."*

I could see some uprooted trees and some destroyed homes. Jesus said: *"My people, in your disasters you are learning a new lesson in helping your neighbor. When you are working for survival from floods, storms or earthquakes, your selfishness and affluence melt away. It is when you are joined in a common cause that you find a true value in friendship. See from this lesson that you can focus on helping others all the time and not just with problems. By stripping your affluence and bringing you to your knees, you are being forced to remember your beginnings when God was more a part of your life. Your country was founded on a reliance on God. It is time to return to your roots."*

Friday, February 13, 1998:

After Communion, I could see a gyroscope next to the globe of the earth. Jesus said: *"My people, the earth now is anything but stable. You have abused the air, the water and the land to the point where the earth is reacting on its own. You do not realize how delicate a balance that your ecosystems are in. I allowed man to subdue the earth, but not to destroy it. Your pollution is affecting your weather, such that the warmer oceans are causing severe storms from the west. Any potential wars again will endanger your environment either from burning oil wells or dangerous chemicals in the atmosphere. Think before you act about the consequences of what you are doing. This applies to your earthly situation as well as your spiritual life. A well thought out prayer life will reap you a rich harvest of graces. So, look for peace among your nations and your environment before more chastisements befall you."*

Later, at Emmaus Center Adoration Webster, Mass., I could see a small town with some trees planted in a row. Then I saw those trees cut back to near stumps and there was a vision of moving into wooded lots. Jesus said: *"My people, you have grown accustomed to your comforts. A time is coming when your towns will be changed drastically in their appearance. As the tribulation approaches, you will find it more difficult to find a proper Mass and true devotion to Me. Already you are witnessing the apostasy all around you. You will soon have to move into the country for your safety from the evil ones. Have trust in My angels when they will lead you to the safe havens. It is faith in My help that will be needed most and not a reliance on what you can do. Seek My help in all that you do and I will assist you in all of your needs. I will go out of My way to do the impossible, so you can understand how much I love you."*

Saturday, February 14, 1998:

At Our Lady Queen of Martyrs Church, Woonsocket, Rhode Island, after Communion, I could see a dark wooden church. Jesus said: *"My people, many of My faithful have such a deep love for Me, that they would travel many miles to be at a Mass, and receive Me in Holy Communion. I share this opportunity of My graces of My sacraments with all who wish to come and share in My love. You do not always realize how I offer this miracle of My Body and Blood to you each day. Those who attend daily Mass know of My spiritual blessing which I offer to you in My Eucharist. I give you Myself in My Real Presence so you can be a part of Me for others. My friends, I am offering you this blessing for free every day. If some were offered free tickets to a big football game or basketball game, they would be there for sure. But here at Mass you have the greatest gift you could receive and many pass up this golden opportunity for My love and My graces. Treasure My Real Presence at the Mass, for soon you may have difficulty in finding Me at a proper and valid Mass. You will undergo persecution in the tribulation, but I will always grace you with My Heavenly Manna through My angels in Spiritual Communion. I will not leave you orphans, but I will be with you in My Presence until the end of time."*

Later, at Emmaus Center Adoration, Webster, Mass., I was outside looking at the poles and a telephone receiver could be seen. Jesus said: *"My people, you have let phones and paging devices run your life. You even take them in your cars. There are times when calls are necessary, but you have raised your use of electronic devices to a new level of dependency. All these devices have enabled you to do, is speed up your business. You raise your living to such an intensity that this stress of things occupies your mind with too many earthly concerns. You have consumed your time with your fast-living so much that you have little time for Me. It is better for you to calm down your activity to a slower pace, so you can appreciate the beautiful things going on in your life. Take time more to be with your family in conversing with them, than building your life up with too many activities. Take time for your prayer life as well. Knowing Me is the most important part of your life, but you cannot show Me your love if you are racing through life as a race driver. Keep close to Me in your thoughts each day and do not let the devil confuse you with so much activity and distractions."*

Sunday, February 15, 1998:

At Precious Blood Church, Woonsocket, Rhode Island after Communion I could see a laced veil on a wall at a confessional. Jesus said: *"My people, in this life you are in a valley of tears. You all are faced with the trials and difficulties of life. In your sins you would be lost, if I did not die on the cross for you. But as it is, I did redeem you and your joy should be complete. I am showing you the confessional where I call you to voice your sins under the veil of secrecy in Confession. As the priest hears your sins, they are placed far from Me. Come to Me in sorrow and contrition for your sins. All of you are sinners and are in need of*

My forgiveness. Do not despair in your guilt, but come to Me and I will release you from your bonds of sin. Once forgiven, you can rejoice triumphant that you are back in My heavenly graces. A pure heart and soul are most pleasing to Me. Even amidst your weaknesses, you can be cleansed of your sins whenever you visit Me in Confession. I send you forth with My blessings to strengthen you in your struggles with the evil one. I love all of you, My children, and I am here for you in all of your spiritual and physical needs."

Later, at Adoration, I could see a United States warship and next to it was a sand bar with water all around it. Jesus said: *"My people, why does your government insist on carrying out these air strikes? If your country gets involved with a war in Iraq, you could find yourself in a quagmire of trouble and public opinion. There will be division in your own country, and many Arab countries will unite against you. The longer you stay there, the more you will be involved, and the wider other nations might become involved. Pray that your leaders stop this madness and settle your differences peacefully. These foreign ambitions will only cause you more problems, and it will not achieve any of your objectives."*

Monday, February 16, 1998:

After Communion, I could see an inside corner where one could hide. Jesus said: *"My people, you know how the dust collects in the corners and sometimes you would like to hide there for a time to avoid life's trials. Life is too short, my friends, to try and take a respite. It is when you try to get too comfortable that the devil will try to get you off the track to the mission you are called. With each new day, see this as an opportunity to take one more step with Me on your way to Heaven. Instead of seeking a rest, struggle each day to use your talents to the best of your ability. Never look back, but move forward in your work for Me and your neighbor. It is only at the end of the day that you can take stock of how you are doing. Then, with a firm purpose of your assessment, strive to improve on your deeds for the next day. Always keep a positive outlook of faith in where I am leading you, and share My love with all those in your life."*

Later, at Adoration, I could see massive clouds all over the earth. Then Our Lady appeared with the sun shining out from her. Mary said: *"My dear children, peace has been very elusive through the years, as man returns to wars over land. These billows of smoke are the war clouds gathered over the earth. I have asked you for many years to pray that men will come to the table of my Son's peace. If you do not take my Son's peace, your earthly peace will mean nothing. You must live in His love both for yourself and your neighbor. It is a good lesson to walk in my Son's footsteps. Listen to Him in the Gospel, then you would have no wars at all. Those who refuse to want peace will repeat the errors of the past. This confrontation is no different, since hate in war begets more hate in return. Love one another, or your world will be in constant turmoil."*

Tuesday, February 17, 1998:

After Communion, I could see a runway in the dark with planes taking off. Jesus said: *"My people, you have experienced a relative peace for several years. Now, the evil one is trying to arouse hatred between nations once again. Do not be so impulsive to jump right into another attack on Iraq. Stop and see that armed conflict will not accomplish ousting Saddam, nor will it rid all of his weapons. You are being led into this fray under false pretenses and Saddam's taunts. Pray for peace in this situation, because war will not solve the inspection problems. War will only make a bad problem worse. The general people do not want war, it is only the leaders and the media who are hyping it."*

Later, at Adoration, I could see a smoking fire coming up out of the ground. Then all of a sudden it grew dark where the fire had been. Jesus said: *"My people, the evil one is very active now as he is preparing the way for the Antichrist's appearance. This is why you are seeing the fire of Hell reaching out of the ground. At the time of the great tribulation, all of the demons will be roaming the earth in search of souls to destroy. With your prayers and My help, you will be protected. Have faith in Me that I will overcome all of the evil spirits. That is why the flames later went out, as I will conquer all of the evil spirits and place them in Hell. Prepare for the spiritual battle of your life. As you will be tempted in vari-*

ous ways, even My elect will need that time shortened. When Satan is cast into Hell, I will then renew the earth and you will enjoy the Era of Peace on earth."

Wednesday, February 18, 1998: (Funeral Mass)
After Communion, I could see Jesus coming in a white robe as He was rising. Then I saw a white rose followed by a flame burning. Jesus said: *"My dear children, there is life in the spirit after death. It is only the body that passes on, your soul continues because it is immortal. At the judgment day you will be reunited with your body once again. I am showing you this white rose as a symbol of purity in the love I share with all of mankind. It is also a symbol of love that you have for Me and your neighbor. You will be judged on how you loved Me and the extent that you loved your neighbor. The flame, I am showing you, is how you will live forever in your spirit. It is how you lived that will determine whether you stay with Me in Heaven or with Satan in Hell. Be always ready for your death, for you know not the hour that I will call you home. Pray with Me each day and have your soul in sanctifying grace by frequent Confession. Then your soul will be ready to make your transition from time into the eternal now."*

Thursday, February 19, 1998:
After Communion, I could see some pews in a church and they had some comfortable reclining seats. Jesus said: *"My people, you have become too relaxed in your worship at Mass and you give My Real Presence little respect. You must struggle to preserve the proper words of the Mass, especially those of the Consecration. Also, many are receiving Holy Communion in mortal sin which is a sin of sacrilege against My Body and Blood of this sacrament. Your souls must be properly purified by Confession or in a state of grace in order to receive your Lord in Holy Communion. St. Peter did not want Me to die for your sins, but you must be ready to think of following My Divine Plan instead of your earthly ways. Your life on earth is always tested with suffering as well as the happy things. As you approach the great tribulation you will have to suffer even the Mass being taken away from you. A religious persecution will come over your land when you will have to*

have underground Masses. As the priests will be hard to find, you will be left with only Spiritual Communion. But I will bless you in those days with My Heavenly Manna, so that I will be with you still in My Real Presence. Trust in My help and keep strong in your faith and you will win your salvation."*

Later, at the prayer group, I could see a log across a stream. The stream started as a trickle and it built up into a raging river. Jesus said: *"My people, I am the bridge across your troubled waters. You are being tested by continuing rain storms and a warmer climate. Your streams will grow swollen again as the rain will continue to batter your country. See that your sins need cleansing and when your things are stripped, you will see Me more clearly."*

I could see a train in a tunnel and bombs going off at the entrances to these tunnels. Jesus said: *"My people, this struggle that you are having in deciding to go to war is very precarious. If your military tries to destroy these toxic weapons, it could unleash many poisons into the air that could get out of control. If man does not destroy these weapons, they will be used in a desperate hour. Pray for peace now, because the fallout of this war may be out of control and spread to other nations."*

I was in an underground dwelling and there was a golden opening in the ceiling and a great light shone out from it. Jesus said: *"My people, never forget that I alone have power over all that is in the universe. Any seeming power of the evil one is being allowed as a test for you. There will come a day after the tribulation when I will come on a cloud in all glory and splendor. It is then that Satan and his minions will be cast into Hell. Then I will renew the earth for you to show you Heaven on earth."*

I could see a bright sun and it became eclipsed by the moon. In that darkness there was a reddish pink whirlwind that came forth. Jesus said: *"My dear children, after the eclipse of the sun, you will see a whirlwind of events that man is calling down on himself. The wider these events become, the broader the scope of these events will be. Pray much, My people, for these events could trigger the declaration of the Antichrist. When the spirits of darkness come on the earth, there will be a tremendous battle leading up to that at Armageddon in Israel. This will be the final and mother of all battles. For this will be a conflict of all the good against all that is evil."

I could see a cross in the darkness and people were kneeling in sackcloth and ashes. Jesus said: *"My people, as Lent begins on Ash Wednesday, you will be praying long hours on your knees that this proposed conflict will not start or that it will come to a swift end. For if this war is prolonged, it will increase the chances of a wider conflict and possibly World War III. Pray continually to mitigate any nuclear or chemical weapons being used. If you could see what war lies at stake, you would be on your knees day and night."*

I could see a construction vehicle in yellow and black stripes coming from a dark tunnel. Jesus said: *"My people, if a wider war is imminent, I will let My angels lead you to some caves or they will make them for you. You may need such protection from any fallout or bomb surges. If atomic weapons are used, you could see the nuclear winter caused by the debris in the sky. You may need to protect your water from any contamination. Pray, my people, as you have never prayed before, for man's very existence will hang in the balance. Stop your wars of madness or you will not be able to hold back these chastisements."*

I could see Mary come and there was a white star that was burning with flames. Mary said: *"My dear children, I have told you at Fatima that unless there were enough prayer, you could see several nations annihilated. You are slowly coming to a turning point in this prophecy. If you do not storm Heaven with a daily barrage of my Rosaries, you may witness a nuclear attack. I have told you often to pray my Fifteen Decade Rosary for peace. Now, it is becoming more apparent why this prayer is so needed to balance the evil in your world. Pray that my Son's hand will intervene before man destroys himself."*

Friday, February 20, 1998:

After Communion, I could see a cross in the night. Then, I could see Jesus' Body on the cross. Jesus said: *"My dear children, it is important for you to remember that you have been redeemed by My Blood on the cross. I am the Divine Sacrifice where I suffer for all of your sins. This is why it is so important for you to *only use a crucifix with My Suffering Body. A cross without My Body has no sense of suffering. Even the crosses of My Resurrection are missing the point of My Redemption of all of mankind. Again in the reading, it is important to have faith and good works if you are to be saved. Those who only cry Lord, Lord, and have no works in their hands, I will tell them that I do not know them. You need more than just a head knowledge of the faith. Faith without love is nothing at all. You must show Me your love as well as your love of neighbor in your works. Without the Corporal Works of Mercy, how can I see that you truly love Me? Those who have no works are committing the greatest sin of omission that they could. If you truly love Me, you will help your neighbor in his need. For when you help your neighbor, you are helping Me as well. I am present in every soul, so when you look at each person you are looking at Me. This is why those who do not help others are not loving me as well."*

Later, at St. Clemens' Adoration, Toronto, Ontario, Canada, I could see a service man and he opened a gate to let a car go through. Jesus said: *"My son, the evil one is attacking your thoughts because of the good that you are doing in leading souls back to Me. You will see more of these attacks evident as you influence more and more souls to repentance. Many know the way to follow Me, but they allow the evil one to distract them with their comforts. Come, My faithful, and have faith that I will protect you in all of your conflicts. Your battles with the evil one will become increasingly difficult, but I will subdue him."*

Saturday, February 21, 1998:

After Communion, I could see some old people in the pews at church. Jesus said: *"My people, you see many older faithful in church, but there are few of My younger children attending Mass. If your faith is to live on, it must be passed on to your children. If you do not teach your children the faith and do not encourage them to attend Mass, how will My Church live on? When you know the Gospel, you must share it with others, especially your own family. Do not be afraid to disturb their peace, but give them good example by your own attendance at Mass. Pray for your children and teach them My love. It is your responsibility to bring these souls to Me. They will decide for Me on their own, but you must educate them in the faith, so they can make a proper decision. The innocent souls of the children need to be brought to a knowledge of Me. Do not leave this important work to chance, but let them be led to My love in the Mass."*

Sunday, February 22, 1998:

At the Church of the Infant Jesus, Ottawa, Ontario, Canada, after Communion, I could see a living Trinity in a triangle with sunlight shining through it. Then a picture of God the Father was shown. God the Father said: *"I AM comes to you, My children, for I have created you all in My image to know, love and serve Me. By Adam's fall you are all weak in your sins and in need of repentance. I have sent you My Son as a sin offering to atone for all of mankind's sin. You, for your part, must acknowledge that you are sinners and seek true forgiveness of your sins through My Son in the priest at Confession. Come to Me out of love with sorrow in your heart for your transgressions against Me. All souls all over the world have to recognize Me as God over their lives and I alone am worthy of your worship. I will send you the warning so that everyone will know who their God is, and they will know what true good and evil are. Then they will no longer be able to say that I do not exist, and they will be responsible for seeking Me for the forgiveness of their sins. All those who fail to seek this cleansing of their sins will be the deadest of the dead, for the unfaithful will endure an eternity in Hell. Come, My lovely ones, and share in the glory of Heaven that has been reserved for all of My chosen ones. After this life in this age, I will re-create the world again with no evil in My sight, as all the evil ones will be cast into Hell. Enjoy My new Jerusalem on earth as your final preparation for Heaven."*

Later, at Marmora, Ontario, Canada, I could see Our Lady in blue and white as in flight moving and pointing to the hill above the Greenside's house. Mary said: *"My dear children, I am calling you to the hill area as a place of holy ground. I will be watching over this area even during the tribulation. Many will flock here as a special sharing of my presence. It is beautiful for pilgrims to visit my holy ground places, since you will receive my graces for your faith. Even in your own homes, you can visit me, when you pray my Rosary. I am a heavenly mother for all of my children and I ask you to seek my abundant graces wherever you are. Consecrate yourselves to the two hearts of Jesus and myself.*

It is by praying and living your consecration that you will be protected and saved. Live in love of me and my Son, Jesus, and your heart will be filled with a joy that no one can take from you. Pray and have trust in Jesus that you will be guided to Heaven by following in His footsteps."

Monday, February 23, 1998:

After Communion, I could see a dark casket on a stand. Jesus said: *"My people, when you see somebody dead in a casket, it should be a reminder to you that one day you will face this same fate. Once you die, you cannot change how you will be judged. That is why whenever you are in mortal sin, it is important to seek forgiveness in Confession. If you do not repent of your sins, you could find yourself in Hell for eternity. See that keeping your soul cleansed from sin is your most important task. It is better to avoid any such serious sin in the first place. But if you fall, pick yourself up again. Do not wallow in your sin or get spiritually lazy and forget your prayers. Encourage all those around you to frequent Confession. Many souls are lost because no one has witnessed Me to them or no one has prayed for their souls. While a soul is alive, they are capable of being saved. So, help these souls wake up spiritually before it is too late."*

At Adoration, I could see a large desert with a long straight road running through it. Jesus said: *"My people, the desert represents how you are tested in life. You sometimes become dry in your faith, only to visit My Blessed Sacrament as an oasis in the desert. I went out to pray in the desert many times where the quiet enabled Me to hear My Father. It was also in the desert where the evil one tempted Me. You are about to start your forty days in the desert with your Lenten services. Use this time to repent of your sins, and make a firm purpose of amendment to follow My commands, and keep on the straight and narrow road to Heaven. You need a desert experience to know that this life is one of suffering and not one of pleasure. Follow in My footsteps of carrying your cross through Lent. By acts of self-denial and other means of fasting, you can train your body and soul to follow My Divine Will in all you do. By living up to your consecration, you will lose your desire for this world's pleasures and seek instead to be with My Divine Love. Love Me and your neighbor unconditionally and you will be on your straight road to Heaven."*

Tuesday, February 24, 1998: (Joe Trunfio's Funeral Mass)
After Communion, I could see some children and behind them there was an empty tomb. After, I could see Joe alive and he was carrying a silver vessel and lifting it up to God. Jesus said: *"My people, I have found favor in My son, Joseph. His witness to you has been a grace to the family and a symbol of faith for all of you to follow. You are witnesses that there is only one God before you, even though you raise many idols of earthly worship. My love and My mercy are poured out over all of My children, for you each have the indwelling of the Holy Spirit. Go before Me and share My love among all of your neighbors and friends. Love is life because I have created it so. It is this same love that I am asking you to return to Me in praise and worship. So, as Lent approaches, you too, are asked to carry your crosses of suffering. Give of yourself generously both to me and your neighbor. It is this love you have that will be your judgment, when one day I will call each of you home."* (Joe was a 35 year old family man whose acceptance of his terminal condition was an inspiration to everyone.)

Later, at Adoration, I could see a clock and a rat running on a wheel. Jesus said: *"My people, come to me in your trials and I will grant you My peace. When you come into the presence of My Blessed Sacrament, I put your soul at rest. Let all the distractions of the day leave you, as you sit down to pray. If you are still distraught, pray a prayer to Me to take away your outside thoughts. You need a clear mind to listen to Me. Many of My children are wrapped up in too many activities. Always make time for prayer in your life. If you find difficulty in making prayer time, go back and analyze each hour of the day to see if you are wasting time. Time is a precious gift that I give to each soul. It is up to you to manage your time for the best interest of your soul. A prayerful person has much peace about them, since they are confident in doing My Will. When you do everything for Me, you will see that all you do is a labor of love. When you visit the sick and comfort the mourning, you are comforting Me in them. The more you help your neighbor, the more graces you are storing up in Heaven. Strive* for these heavenly treasures instead of worrying about your earthly treasures. Love is your goal and sharing your time and money with others, shows me that you are not selfish. Continue these good works in your life, and you will receive a heavenly reward."

Wednesday, February 25, 1998: (Ash Wednesday)
After Communion, I could look up from the bottom of a tall skyscraper with all of its lights. I then saw the Lincoln Memorial and the Statue of Liberty. Jesus said: *"My people of America, you have squandered your inheritance with your corrupt living, and your Towers of Babel will be brought low. The decadence of your morals and your disregard for life calls down My justice, as you will face many chastisements. The storms of violence that are exacting their toll on you are just an example of how your wealth will be stripped from you. Your greed for money and material things will bring you bankruptcy in your spiritual laziness. Your freedoms that you have taken for granted for so many years will be taken away from you, since you have not fought for them. You have sought nothing but pleasure and money while your spiritual life is in rags. My people of America need to wake up this Lent and repent of your sins, before your civilization falls in ruin. You have all of the signs of a decaying nation and still you do not see your own corruption. When you take God out of your schools and your morals are in the gutter, where do you expect Me to help you? Unless you repent of your sins and change your death culture, you will stagnate to your dying days."*

Later, at Helen Rosenthal's Cenacle Prayer Group, I could see a white outline over every corner of a house. Jesus said: *"My people, I am showing you how My faithful will be meeting in houses for prayer. You will need the power of your prayer groups to endure the coming persecution. Your Masses in the churches will be coming to an end as the schism spreads throughout My Church. Prepare your vessels now for the underground Masses that you will attend. As your priests are going to be hard to find, you will be left only with the Rosary and your Spiritual Communion. I will perform miracles in your midst to bring you My Host by My angels during the tribulation. Stay united in prayer wherever you find each other together and I will protect you from all evil."*

Thursday, February 26, 1998:

After Communion, I could see some penguins moving about as a group. Jesus said: *"My people, there are lessons in life in even the most common of settings. Humans of like mind travel in each other's company very much like some flocks of birds. Many times you want to share your feelings and sufferings with someone who will listen to you and understand. Your prayer groups unite you in a common cause to pray and share life with each other. But do not feel that you are better than anyone else. If you are truly imitating My life, let others recognize you as Christians because of how much you love one another. You need to show this love not only with your prayer group members, but with those in public as well. Then your witness of love will spread among your neighbors and My peace will be spread as well."*

Later, at the prayer group, I could see a soldier with his sword drawn. Jesus said: *"My people, you are witnessing a forced peace in a situation where many arms are still poised for war. This fragile excuse for peace will not last long. Your leaders have a pride in seeking power that may still result in war. As long as each side is not satisfied with the terms of peace, war clouds will hang over this area. Pray much for peace and pray more that the hearts of your leaders will be softened with love and not hardened with hate."*

I could see some purple veils representing the Passion of Jesus during Lent. Jesus said: *"My people, Lent is a time when you can profit by your contrition for sin and your resolution to bear your sufferings for Me. Continue in your acts of self-denial to curb the body in its desire for food and pleasure. Count each day of these forty days with a desire for constant prayer and following My Will. When you make a good Lent, your spiritual life will be uplifted. Struggle each day in your Lenten devotions. Take time to do My Stations each day of Lent."*

I could see some signs of a court room. Jesus said: *"My people, your justice system has many cracks in its motives. Your lawyers are quick to pursue litigation over the least problem even when the accused are only passively involved. It is more out of greed for money that cases are carried out. In the end, the results of your justice are worked out in back room deals instead of true justice."*

I could see some women and children suffering without homes and food. Jesus said: *"My people, look on the poor innocent victims of your wars and the chastisements falling with your weather. Pray for those displaced from their homes and help them with your money in providing food and clothing. Share your abundance with those less fortunate, as you need to give your alms this Lent."*

I could see a crucifix covered with a purple cloth. Jesus said: *"My people, your traditions of days past showed real signs for you in your preparation for Lent. In those days you had statues to cover, but now your statues have been removed. It is good to have remembrances of the lives of the saints before you. You need to have good examples of spiritual heroes to emulate. Without thoughts of leading clean spiritual lives, how can you come to Heaven?"*

I could see an image of St. Michael the Archangel subduing Satan. St. Michael was given permission to speak and he said: *"I am Michael and I stand before God. I am also guardian over your country, but many do not want to believe in angels. We protect you daily in ways you never know. Give thanks to God that we are allowed to assist you. When you call on our help, we will be at your side to subdue the evil spirits. When you commit serious sin, you deprive us of helping you. So, reach out for frequent Confession so you can be restored to the beautiful souls that you were meant to be."*

I could see some flooded crop lands. Jesus said: *"My people, look to the trials of your weather chastisements. Already you will see signs of increased prices for your food. In addition, you should notice that it may be even in short supply. You have had to suffer some short losses in your electricity, but when food shortages and more diseases afflict you, you will then experience the coming famine and pestilence. Pray much, My children, for you will have to suffer much to cleanse your sins and the temporal punishment due for them."*

Friday, February 27, 1998:

At the Assumption of the Blessed Virgin Mary Church, Miami, Florida, after Communion, I could look down the aisle of a church and see Jesus in the Blessed Sacrament. Jesus said: *"My people, all of those who are faithful to My Name have the same true God, no matter which rite that you share. Come to Me in My Blessed Sacrament, for in Me you have My Real Presence. Even for those who do not accept My Body and Blood in the bread and wine as My Real Presence, I am still there. I gave My life as a Divine Sacrifice for you in reparation for your sins. In Me you find your redemption. Never leave Me or you will be lost. Visit Me in My Blessed Sacrament to honor and worship Me. Give Me thanks and give Me your petitions. I love all of you so much. So, come share in My love, for today and tomorrow you are the branches that are a part of My Mystical Body."*

Saturday, February 28, 1998:

At the Assumption of the Blessed Virgin Mary Church, Miami, Florida, after Communion, I could see a door to Heaven opening and all the glory of Heaven was shown forth. There at the gate Pope John Paul II was leading us. Jesus said: *"My people, I am showing you how My pope son, John Paul II, is leading My flock to Heaven. Listen to him in every decree and instruction and make it a part of your life. Never doubt My power that I will watch over My Church, even during the tribulation. The Church is led by My Pope John Paul II, and do not listen to any other who claims to be Me. I am the one God you are to follow and worship. Give no allegiance to any other than Me. My faithful follow the true teachings and traditions of My Magisterium. Never deviate from the gift of My Apostles. False witnesses will come claiming to be Me or claiming you should worship them. Do not believe this Antichrist and follow only Me and Pope John Paul II and no other. My glory will be shown you soon when I come on the clouds to share My triumph with all of mankind. Be ever faithful and trust in My help and protection."*

Later, at Clearwater, Florida, by the image of Our Lady of Guadalupe on the windows of an office building. Mary said: *"My dear children, I have given you many signs and messages of my presence and still many do not believe. Thank you for visiting my image in witness to my coming in this place. No matter how much man tries to distort my image, it still remains. Instead of trying to deny my messages, my children need to be praying more on their knees for my intentions. I am dressed in the sun by the rainbow so you can understand how important it is to stop your abortions. The closing of this abortion clinic is another sign of what prayer can achieve. I have told you many times, that if enough prayer is said in America, I will bring your abortions to a halt. Also, you*

need to pray much for peace in your world. If you do not heed my invitation for prayer in these intentions, I will not be able to hold back my Son's hand in His justice. Your killing of the babies and those innocent in war represents the evil that needs to be cleansed in your world. Jesus will no longer permit you to destroy the life that He has created. Pray, pray, pray more, my children, while you still have time. It is not difficult to pray. You must move your will to understand the need for all of this prayer. There is a scale of good weighed against evil and the scales are not being tilted toward the good. My Son, Jesus suffers much for your sins. Please confess your sins and refrain from further sin. Your heavenly mother is pleading with you to do good and discourage these evil killings in abortion."

Sunday, March 1, 1998:

At St. Charles Borromeo Church in Port Charlotte, Florida, after Communion, I could see some public baths and I understood that we are in constant need of cleansing our sins. Jesus said: *"My people, as St. John the Baptist sought to baptize and cleanse the sins of sinners, I come seeking to cleanse your sins in the Sacrament of Reconciliation. You all are in want of My forgiveness and you need My graces to seek your salvation. See in the readings how you are tempted in sin. Look to your own life as you may be worshiping the idols of the earth more than Me. How you spend your time is how you worship your idols. You need to be on your knees praying for My mercy for your sins. Many spend their time worshiping your gods of money and entertainment. Seek Me first and I will provide what you need. Do not be worried about what you will eat or what you are to wear. Concentrate your attention on following My Will and the Devil will have difficulty in tempting you with the desires of the world. With your focus on Me only, you will not have time for worldly things. Strive to gain heavenly treasures and your soul will be completely satisfied in My peace."*

Monday, March 2, 1998:

After Communion, I could see some people standing in a dingy brown house with no colors. Jesus said: *"My people, do not hold back doing good deeds because of your pride or your selfishness. Even if you must go to unpleasant places of dirt and poverty places, reach out to the poor where they are and help them. When you have more than you need, do not worry whether you have enough for yourself, but share what you have with others. I tell you, what little you give, will be multiplied beyond your need. Be willing to share your time in helping the needy. When you share your time, money, or goods, you are sharing them with Me. So, do not hold back in your giving, but give generously without concern of any loss. For you will gain heavenly treasures that will far surpass any earthly value of what you give. Share your faith with others as well, because those you can bring to My Gospel, may be brought back to My graces. Saving souls, after all, should be your highest calling."*

Later, at Adoration, I could see some violent cartoons. Jesus said: *"My people, you have seen your movies exploited for money, but now even those things made for the children are poisoning these little minds with evil. With the weather I have lashed the places of your movie making both in California and Florida. I have given them many such warnings of near destruction. If they persist in their guile and abuse of your entertainment, I will soon destroy their places of business. I have allowed many beautiful miracles to bring encouragement in your faith. You need to be looking for these signs both in the heavens and among your ordinary things. See by these signs that you are drawn to change your lives. The spirit of Lent is to renew your spiritual life by your many Lenten devotions. Most important is to have your sins confessed frequently. Be conscious that you need to be always ready for when I will call your soul home. These forty days should be a special preparation in prayer, fasting, alms-giving, and good deeds for you. Use this time wisely so you can bring yourself closer to My heart. By cleansing your spiritual life with mortification, you can follow My Will more closely."*

Tuesday, March 3, 1998:

After Communion, I could see several purses in a row. Jesus said: *"My people, there are some generous people, but there are also many who hold their purses too close. Even those that have enough to get by and those with excesses are reluctant to donate to the poor. They will claim many excuses for not giving, but there are many charities they could find if they tried hard enough. During Lent, giving alms is an old tradition, but few share with others. Do not just give token amounts, but give of your substance and I will know that you have true love of Me in your heart. Give to those causes most where you will get nothing in return. Your money in time will do you no good. Donate it now to charities and you can exchange your earthly gifts for heavenly treasures. When you give, do not let your left hand know what your right hand is doing. Do not look for glory on earth in your giving, or you will have already been repaid. What you give in secret, your Father will see and repay you abundantly."*

Note: We took our three-year old granddaughter to Adoration.

Later, at Adoration, I could see St. Therese with some roses and she was prostrate on the floor. St. Therese said: *"My little ones, it is good to bring the children to experience Jesus in the Blessed Sacrament. Do not keep the children from Mass, even if they are hard to manage. It is by your good example that you bring the young children with you to adore Jesus. You must be like the innocent children, free of pride and fear. Come to Jesus freely and be open with your Lord and accept Him into your heart. He loves you and the children very much. So, always bring them to Him and show Him your love, so the children will see your love for Jesus."*

Wednesday, March 4, 1998: (Jonah readings)

After Communion, I could see a water hose wound up neatly on a circular holder. Jesus said: *"My people, you need to struggle each day to stay close to Me. This watering device shows you how you are in need of constant cleansing of your sins. Lent is a time to meditate on your actions and prune out all of your occasions for sin. See by your frequent confessing of your sins that you are constantly cleansing away any evil in your life and replacing it with My graces of the Sacrament of Reconciliation. Lent is a time to repent of your sins as Jonah encouraged those of Nineveh to change their evil ways. Because of your evil age, I am sending you many messengers with this same message of repentance. Your* sins require you to seek forgiveness before the priest in Confession. See this as an excellent time to do your Easter duty of attending Confession at least once during Lent. Do not be afraid to confess your sins, for cleansing your guilt will unload many of your anxieties."

Thursday, March 5, 1998: (Queen Esther)
After Communion, I could see a woman dressed in clothes of an earlier year. Jesus said: *"My people, it is good to read of how women played a role in the history of Scripture. Even though women were held in low esteem for many years, there are many role models of virtue in the Scriptures. Look to follow the lives*

of these women of prayer in how heroic they were for all that they accomplished. As you study the women saints of even recent years, you will see how many spirited women were given to you to lead in difficult times. Instead of complaining about their station in life, these saints were models of hope and faith which the women of today should be proud to imitate. Even in your own time, you have been blessed with many women of faith to lead My people in keeping their faith."

At the prayer group, I could see a light on the outside of a house and it became very dim. Jesus said: *"My people, more and more the evil one is being allowed to test My faithful in even physical things. You have witnessed for yourself how the price of souls requires some suffering of problems. As this evil age approaches the time of the Antichrist, more testing by evil spirits will become commonplace. I tell you, My people, that My power and that of My angels far surpasses anything that the demons may influence. When you witness cold and strange things, sprinkle holy water and place blessed sacramentals in such areas. If a priest is willing, even have this area blessed by the priest. Remember that evil's power pales in comparison to Me. Call on your angels to protect you and remove any signs of the satanic cult."*

I could see some ravens and other signs of the occult. Jesus said: *"My children, beware of the New Age symbols which are satanic sacramentals. Be willing to expose the use of these symbols as satanic and discourage the children from playing with them or carrying these things. The demons use these means to enter areas of their control. Many of these innocent symbols will lead to more influence by the evil ones."*

I could see a house submerged into a raging river. Jesus said: *"My people, your violent storms are not over. You will see continuing problems with flooding and other natural disasters. Many are still blind to the connection of your sins to your chastisements. As more are brought to their knees by being stripped of their riches, man will realize his testing time has come whether he wants to believe it or not."*

I could see a dark factory that was closed up. Jesus said: *"My people, the greed of the rich has set into motion a financial imbalance that will cause many factories to close and the loss of jobs. As this spiral of bankruptcies and money problems continue, you will see a world depression that will offer the Antichrist his opportunity to enter. As chaos from wars and financial disruption increase, the Antichrist will enter as a man of peace to settle your problems. His reign will be one of a tyrant, but it will last only a moment when I will bring my triumph down upon this evil lot."*

I could see a storm of rain and then it stopped and the sun shone brightly. Jesus said: *"My people, just when you think the Antichrist has come to full power, I will bring My light into this world of evil. When I come on the clouds, I will rain down My justice on the evil ones and they will all be cast into Hell. You, My faithful, will then witness My renewed earth and you will see your reward for your faithfulness in living in My Era of Peace. Look forward to this time when evil will be conquered and My light of grace will restore the earth as I originally meant it to be. You will then share in My glory and give praise to Me the Almighty over everything."*

I could see Our Lady and a large dollar bill covered her. Mary said: *"My dear children, do not let your desire for money cloud your thinking. Many mothers are choosing the abortion of their own children for the sake of their comforts or hiding their sins. Pride and the evil one's influence have clouded your minds in lowering your value of life. There is no price that you can put on life, but when you give the doctors their thirty pieces of silver to kill your infants, you will have to live with your guilt. Jesus will forgive your sin, but your sins will corrupt your society. Stop your abortions, my children, because these lives are precious to Jesus and these acts call down my Son's justice on your country. See the evil in your ways and repent by sending many of your Rosaries for my intentions."*

Friday, March 6, 1998:

After Communion, I could see people going into some back rooms for Confession. Jesus said: *"My people, you need to take advantage of the Sacrament of Reconciliation in cleansing your sins. Lent is a time for rooting out your sins and changing your lifestyle. Each soul is responsible for its own actions. It is by your own consent of the will that you give in to sin. So, each of you must accept that you are sinners and take responsibility for your own sin and how to stop sin in your life. The guilt of your sins is removed by absolution in Confession. It is when you violate My Commandments that you are not fair in accepting My love. When you are unfaithful to Me, you are in most need of My cleansing graces. Do not feel that you are alienated from My love, but seek My plenteous forgiveness so your spiritual life can be renewed. Do not be lazy in your sin, but struggle to come back into My light as soon as possible. Do not put off confessing your sins, but go quickly and frequently to Confession to the priest. Then you will feel the full warmth of My love in restoring your soul to the sanctifying grace it seeks."*

Later, at Adoration, I could see an empty room and then a side view of Jesus on the cross. Jesus said: *"My people, at My cross when I was dying, few of My followers came in My support. Even now, when I am available in the Host for your adoration, few come to visit Me. Whenever I am present in daily Mass, Adoration, or Confession, there are opportunities for My graces that only a few receive. When you give of your time to visit Me, I see the love that you have for Me in your heart. Those who refuse to visit Me are passing up opportunities to grow in their spirituality. By adoring My Blessed Sacrament, you are showing Me and those around you that I am a high priority in your life. When you come to Heaven, I will easily recognize those of My faithful. Those who do not recognize My Real Presence will receive a lesser place. The more you share in the love of My Eucharist, the higher I will draw your souls. Live to share in My glory, for that is My calling to your soul."*

Saturday, March 7, 1998:

After Communion, I could see Jesus in the Host of the monstrance and His glory was shining over everyone. Jesus said: *"My dear children, My love flows out over you every day like the morning sun. As you come to Mass in the morning, you are infused with My Real Presence in Holy Communion. See the glory and the grace of the union of our spirits. You feel this rush of My love at every Communion. Relax in My rest and share My peace with all of those around you. This love of Mine is to be shared. When you are filled with a measure of My spirit, you are led to share My love with your neighbors. As you reach for this perfection in true love, you are to love your enemies and your persecutors as well. Pray for each soul you meet, that by your example they may learn to love Me also. My love is so overflowing that you will wish to bring everyone to know this love of the Spirit. Give praise to Me in adoration and your soul will have its rest in My Spirit."*

Later, at Adoration, I could see a badge without any markings on it and a man with dark glasses came forward wearing this badge. Jesus said: *"My people, you will see a time when you will be under the rule of a police state to prevent terrorism. As your present justice system will soon collapse under the burden of its own injustices, you will see the pendulum swing to the right in order to correct the chaos. In accepting the tyranny of the Antichrist, you will be giving up your freedoms. This artificial peace will be turned into an absence of God and a religious persecution of those believing in My Name. You will flee into hiding to escape forced internment for your belief. You will need to pray to Me for help in providing for your needs. Do not accept the Mark of the Beast or worship its image. Those, who take the easy way out will be condemned for their idol worship. Those who remain faithful to Me will see their reward in My Era of Peace. Choose life with Me instead of death with the Antichrist."*

Sunday, March 8, 1998:

After Communion, I could see some children and then the people in the pews. Jesus said: *"My people, cherish the children for the gifts of life that you are being graced with. This is the next generation of the faithful which brings a heavy responsibility for you to pass on the traditions of My Church intact to them. When you teach the children and bring them to the Mass, do not confuse them with modernism nor change the words of the Mass. Teach them respect for My Real Presence and have them praise and adore Me. Teach them to come to Me for help through your petitions, and to thank Me in answering your prayers. In every way, give them good example in living according to My Will. Do not be hypocrites in teaching them by bad example. When you come to the judgment, I will ask you how you helped your children. Your attempts to help them should be honest and I will reward you accordingly. But, if one should lead one of these little ones astray, you will suffer severely. These little ones are precious in My sight and you need prayer and understanding to bring them to Me."*

Later, at Adoration, I could see a sleek train racing very fast. I saw the same train change to more modern designs in stages. Jesus said: *"My people, as your technology advances, you are developing things that do not even have a use yet. This rapid increase in knowledge is one of the signs of the End Times. The trouble with your technology is that you are using it for weapons of destruction. In other fields, you are using gene technology for things in nature that were never intended. You have a knowledge of things, but not the responsibility to abuse that which was given you in creation. This abuse may lead you to a destruction of the very society that man has taken years to nurture. Pray, My people, that you use My gifts in the way they were intended, not to create your own dream world."*

Monday, March 9, 1998:

After Communion, I could see some white houses destroyed. Jesus said: *"My people, you have seen destruction recently from both war and the weather. This causes an unrest for those displaced from their homes. It is this feeling of being stripped of your earthly things that you should be thinking of this Lent. Sometimes you get complacent when you become too affluent with this world's goods. This stripping process should make you think of how dependent you have become on your conveniences. Start planning more for your future after this life, instead of being focused on acquiring wealth here that will be dispersed in a short time. Learn that the things of earth pass away quickly, while the treasures you store in Heaven last forever."*

Later at Adoration, I could see some dying flowers. Jesus said: *"My people, as you watch the life cycle of the flowers, you see how they last but a short time. My friends, so it is with your life, since it is over in a twinkling of an eye. Treat life as precious and delicate, since it is only gifted to you for a time. You even see some are dying at an early age from disease or a sudden acci-*

dent. *That is why Lent is a proper time to prepare your souls for death, since you know not how long you have to live. To be prepared, you must frequent the confessional to have your sins forgiven. This is the time to be sorry for your sins and seek My forgiveness. By cleansing your soul with the grace of Reconciliation, you will always be ready and watching for My return. Love is beautiful and you need your soul close to My heart seeking always My Divine Love. With a clean and loving soul, you will always be in readiness to come to Me in Heaven. If you only would realize how glorious it is to be in Heaven, you would not leave any chance to be lost in your sin. Pray often, My children, so you can be ever sharing in My love."*

Tuesday, March 10, 1998:
After Communion, I could see a strong winter wind over a flat landscape. Jesus said: *"My people, how long will it take to get your attention? You have seen many unusual storms this year and still you are doing everything as you have. Until you understand your sins, you may continue to endure these sufferings. My love and mercy await you always, but few seek My forgiveness of your sins. Since disasters are all that get your attention in your pocketbook, you can expect more of the same. When you are brought to your knees in prayer, then you will know My Will must be served by all. The day I come in glory on the clouds, all men will bow and bend their knee. Why do you fight the inevitable? My Will will be carried out whether you refuse Me or come to love Me. Those who are faithful I will gather into My barn, while those who are unfaithful will face the unquenchable fires of Gehenna. Come now, My children, for now is the acceptable time."*

Later, at Adoration, I could see a table and there was darkness all about it. Jesus said: *"My people, how little are your minds when you think of Me. Many are caught up in the world seeking honor and glory from men. You spend more time glorifying yourselves than giving Me praise and glory. Your accomplishments here on earth are nothing in the face of My creation. Anything you have done could not be done without My gifts to each of you. You are nothingness before Me, yet you still feel fame should honor how much money you have amassed. No matter how much you come* to possess, it would be nothing if you lost your soul in the process. Put everything in perspective and see, what you think is great, will be gone tomorrow. Only that which is everlasting has any true value. So, seek to give Me all the praise and the glory. Never seek fame and riches for yourself. When you seek Me first, I will bless you with all that you need. Work in love of Me and your neighbor, and you will store up treasures in Heaven far superior to anything on earth. Once you realize the true priorities in life, you will be one step closer to Heaven."*

Wednesday, March 11, 1998:
After Communion, I could see a bush and some of its leaves were falling off in the cold weather. Jesus said: *"My people, as the cold of winter comes over the trees and the bushes, they soon lose their leaves. So it is with the souls who grow cold-hearted and cease loving Me. Without love, your sins condemn you and you become separated from Me. When you have filled your soul so much with self, you leave little room for Me to enter. You need to always be on fire with love for Me and your neighbor. During this Lent, re-ignite that fire of love inside you and cleanse the guilt from your souls. By prayer and fasting, you are drawn closer to Me. See that you need My love to wash away any despair in your heart. When you are open to My leading your life, you become alive again in My love. It is through the sacraments and your self-denial that you are re-united with Me, and the coldness of your sinful hearts is turned into a blazing fire of My love. Keep your hearts open to Me, so I can always show you the way to your salvation in Heaven."*

Thursday, March 12, 1998: (George Albert's Funeral Mass)
After Communion, I could see the base of a cross and then up above the cross I could see Jesus receiving George in a white garment. Jesus said: *"My people, when you see the cross, you know that everyone must pickup their cross and follow Me. George, who I am receiving today at your Mass, has followed My way and he has earned his reward for being faithful. He has been a model for all to follow. Be thankful for the gift of his life that I am calling back now. I have promised all mankind in the reading

that those, who eat My Body and drink My Blood, will have eternal life. Your life on earth is very short. But, you have enough time to make your decision to follow Me. Those who seek Me in My sacraments are graced with My love and peace which will never leave My faithful. Those who refuse Me in favor of the idols of this world, I will not recognize before My Father. Choose your direction in life everyday by affirming your love and faith in Me. Trust in My love and help even in the moment of your death. Call on My Name, and I will protect you from all evil."

Later, at the prayer group, I could see a large Host up above the earth with rays of light shining out. Then I saw Jesus in place of the Host. Jesus said: *"My people, I am King of the Universe and everything that happens is guided by My hand. I told you, you would see signs in the sky and events that would quickly fall one after the other. By these eclipses and objects in your sky, you have been given many omens of those things to come. Do not be fearful, My sons and daughters, for I will protect your souls from evil. Your soul should be seeking help more than just for the survival of the body. Your soul will always live on. It is you who will determine your destination."*

I could see a brown wooden angel statue. Mark, my guardian angel, was given permission to speak and said: *"I stand before God and I am to guard you every day. See that all of the angels will be helping you during the tribulation, so have no fear. You are all called to give glory and praise to God as we do. You will soon be tested by an evil time that you have yet to see. This trial will demand your full trust in Jesus throughout the tribulation. Fight with your holy sacramentals, and you will win the battle. Jesus will bring His triumph in His time, but it may come sooner than this latest asteroid. Do not be deluded that there is a long time until the tribulation, for it can start anytime. Be always ready with your daily prayers."*

I could see some bacteria or germs multiplying. Jesus said: *"My people, your diseases will begin to multiply and many will fall sick and die. Some of your outbreaks will be caused by man and some by nature. You will see a pestilence of disease grow across your nation and other nations. Many will die before cures will be found. There will be little defense from these sicknesses, as they will die out as quickly as they came."*

I could see a volcano and red hot lava was flowing out. Jesus said: *"My people, you will see a gradual increase in volcanic activity, and there will be earthquakes associated with these happenings. All of these disturbances are occurring so man will learn how little he controls. The demons will be coming up out of these pits of fire as the tribulation begins. Without My help, you will not survive, so call on My angels to protect you. You will be severely tested, but not beyond your endurance."*

I could see some helicopters in formation over a large city. Jesus said: *"My people, as the evil one begins to take over, you will see these helicopter gun ships take a more active role. You, My people, I have warned to go into hiding before the Antichrist comes into power. I will send you My angels in miraculous ways to protect you. Still, there will be some martyred for belief in My Name. With trust in My help, your souls will be saved, but you may have to suffer some hard environments and persecution."*

I could see a large flame and a crucifix with a corpus. Jesus said: *"My people, see by this flame that the Holy Spirit will protect your spirits with a burning love for you. A blessed crucifix will protect you from evil spirits. Always keep one with you, especially during the tribulation. Sprinkle your holy water as well, and these spirits will leave. I have given you all of the spiritual weapons that you will need. It is up to you to use them in faith."*

I could see some people walking in a shelter and Mary was shielding them with her mantle. Mary said: *"My dear children, I have asked for your prayers for peace in your world and you have been given a reprieve from immediate war. You need to continue in your prayers for tensions are still ready to boil over in many spots in the world. You need to be seeking my Son's peace through love, rather than man's peace by weapons in a stalemate. God loves you so much, yet still your anger and differences continue. Peace in your families is needed most. Without peace in the home, how can you have peace among nations?"*

Friday, March 13, 1998:

After Communion, I could see Jesus with a crown of thorns suffering on the cross. Jesus said: *"My people, in today's read-*

ings you are reminded how Joseph was sold into slavery for twenty pieces of silver. This was a parallel to My betrayal for thirty pieces of silver. In your world, you are selling out your babies for the same thirty pieces of silver. The exact price might be different, but you have cheapened life by putting a price on the heads of your children. It is your doctors, who accept this blood money, that are partners in your crime. How long will you continue to destroy My creations? The chastisements in your weather and an increasing pestilence is being brought on your nation by your sins of abortion. This is the real death row that has not been given any stays of execution. As you look at My suffering on the cross, think of all the future infants being slain before Me. Their angels cry out for justice in front of My glory. It is those committing these sins that are calling down your condemnation. Pray for these mothers to save their children from the butcher's knife."

Later, at the Seven Dolores of Our Lady Parish Center Adoration, Manhattan, Kansas, I could see a Host in a monstrance followed by a modern looking image of Jesus on the cross. Jesus said: *"My people, those who visit Me in adoration of My Blessed Sacrament are blessed with the abundant graces that I bestow on My believers. There are many who may ridicule you as 'bread worshipers' and other derogatory terms, but do not listen to them. Those who criticize My adorers are not giving Me proper respect, or they do not even believe in My Real Presence. I have given you many miracles of the Eucharist to show you that I am truly present in the consecrated Host. I have revealed to you in My Scriptures that My Body and Blood are present in the Host. Those who eat My Body and drink My Blood will have eternal life. Those who fail to believe in My Real Presence are questioning the very roots of their faith. Once you lose a sense of the sacred in My Host, how can you truly come to know and love Me? I have blessed you with this special presence of Mine and I have promised to be with you until the end of time. I will not desert My faithful, but you must discard this modernism that only gives Me lip service. You must make Me personally present in your life every day, if you are to serve Me and follow My Will."* (See John 6:48-58)

Saturday, March 14, 1998: (Prodigal Son)

At Seven Dolores of Our Lady Church, Manhattan, Kansas, after Communion, I could see Jesus in a castle waiting to receive all those who loved Him. Jesus said: *"My people, I call all sinners back to Me in the Sacrament of Reconciliation. Come to Me, My children, no matter how serious your sin and I will forgive you. I will pardon you even until the eleventh hour at the twilight of your life. But come, do not despair in your sin or think yourself unworthy of My forgiveness. Reach out even now to be saved from your sins. My love touches everyone, as I love you unconditionally. For every soul that is brought back, there is rejoicing in Heaven. My faithful that have been with Me from the start, do not be jealous of My generosity to even the most grievous of sinners. I love all of My children equally and you will receive your reward for your generosity of spirit as well. Do not just keep My love to yourself, but share My love with all of those around you. You are My hands and feet, so reach out with My love to bring these sinners back into My sheepfold. For I search constantly for all of My lost sheep and I am happy for every soul that turns from their evil ways to accept Me into their hearts. Love Me always, and give praise to your Lord who awaits to greet you every morning."*

Later, at St. Rose Campus Adoration, Great Bend, Kansas, I could see some yellow streaks in the sky and then the earth orbiting out in space around the sun. Jesus said: *"My people, in recent years you have been visited by both comets and asteroids. Most of the asteroids come from your own solar system, while the comets come from outside your solar system. Comets, with their fuzzy tails, can be seen from greater distances. I have told you the scientists may not tell you of the comet coming to you soon. With all of the close calls you have had recently, you have been prepared for the worst. You still will never be ready for such a collision, but know when My great chastisement comes, man will not be able to change it. These are things meant to be in My plan, as I will cleanse the evil from the earth. People thought this could not happen, but other events have shown the possibility that this could happen very easily. Know, My friends, that when you see the sky falling in on you, that My triumph will soon be here. See that your time of renewal on the earth will bring you a peace that you have yet to experience. Pray much for strength to endure your trials."*

Sunday, March 15, 1998:

At Seven Dolores of Our Lady Adoration, Manhattan, Kansas, I could see an ornate little chapel and inside a tomb area as at the Holy Sepulcher Church in Jerusalem. I then saw a bright light as

when Our Lord resurrected. Jesus said: *"My children, you know that I love you all so much that I died for all of your sins. No greater love can a man have for another than when he offers up his life for him. You are seeing in the tomb the ray of energy that flashed My image into the Holy Shroud. This is the promise of new life with Me that I promise to all that are faithful to My Name. Your souls are immortal, and I offer you a hope and trust in Me that I will raise your body in the same manner. Even if you must suffer the pain of death, you will know that your soul lives on in Me. The body may decay and corrupt, but your soul has a future that you must decide for your destination. Believe in My Easter Resurrection and you can share one day in My glorious return. On that final day of judgment, My faithful will be raised up triumphant in their glorified bodies. When you focus your life on doing My Will, this is your reward that you may see your Lord in Heaven forever."*

At Seven Dolores of Our Lady Church, Manhattan, Kansas, after Communion, I could see a tall, white wall and a young lady walking down a hill with a beautiful blue sky. Jesus said: *"My people, I am showing you the walls that you sometimes build up between your neighbors. By your pride, your need for privacy, and your feeling of independence, you sometimes forget to show your love for your neighbor. Today is a new day in the sun, so that you may tear down these walls of fear and become a loving neighbor. To those around you, reach out to everyone and share that inner love I give each of you. Do not be selfish with your time and money, but share them also with those in need. When you tear down these walls to your neighbor, you are tearing down any walls to Me of your isolation. Tear down all of your earthly idols that you place before Me, and worship Me only in the use of your time. Do not let the worldly things distract you from following My plan for you. In this time of Lent, reform your lives so you can reach out in love for Me and your neighbor. Without love, everything you do is empty. So, put on the gifts of the Spirit and go forth to greet your brothers and sisters."*

Later, at Ascension Church Adoration, Overland Park, Kansas, I could see a large white and green cross indicating Ireland. There were many angels flying around. Jesus said: *"My children, you have been sharing your faith experiences with each other, especially with those you have met in Ireland. You all have realized the beautiful faith that you have had a chance to receive through the nuns and your parents. As you shared, you all desired to share that faith experience with others. You realized, also, how each life is a gift to be shared, since you may never see these people again. But, for a moment, you relived that sharing in faith you first had with each other. The angels I am showing you, are those I send to comfort and protect you in your work. Your work is precious and I am guiding you and those who invite you, so many souls will be enlightened by the words that I bring to you. Give thanks to Me and thank the angels for helping you. In all of your work, many blessings are poured out on you and your sponsors for the beautiful work you are doing to save souls. Continue in your visitations to bring strength to all of My faithful and encourage them in their prayer groups."*

Monday, March 16, 1998:

After Communion, I could see a lot of people at a fancy theater. Jesus said: *"My dear son, do not look for any fame or recognition when you speak. Continue to give your time freely for My service wherever I call you to go. You will be increasingly persecuted for proclaiming My Gospel. Do not have any fear in teaching My Word, but continue in your work for as long as you can spread My message. Many of My prophets have been tortured and killed, but I will give you what to say and do when you are tested. Remain true to My call and give good example by a prayerful life. All of the things that I have given you to do are necessary for a proper spiritual life."*

Later, at Adoration, I could see a large, long hill and many people were walking up the hill. When the people arrived at the top of the hill, I could see the three crosses of Calvary. Jesus said: *"My people, Moses led the Israelites through the desert to the Promised Land. You are seeing the faithful people being led through the desert of Lent to the hill of Calvary. Since Adam's sin, man has been a victim of his own sins. By My example, I have shown you that suffering is a core part of being a Christian. Look to My life as an example to you. You must follow My Commandments and suffer the insults and jeering from the world. My ways are not your ways and you must suffer as I did, if you are to enjoy the promise of My Resurrection. You suffer because your body is always in conflict with the spirit. You cannot gain Heaven on your own. I have conquered sin and death by My dying on the cross. It is My victory that will help carry you up the hill to Heaven. Carry your cross this Lent so you can prepare yourself for that Easter morning, when one day you will be raised up with Me. Come follow My road to Calvary, and you will then be brought to My banquet by your following My Divine Will."*

Tuesday, March 17, 1998: (St. Patrick's Feast Day)

After Communion, I could see several bishops together with their miters. Jesus said: *"My people, you pray for many of your own petitions, but you should also remember to pray for your bishops and priests. Your shepherds have a heavy responsibility for the souls under their care. As the apostles led their little flocks, so it is important for your bishops to lead the people to Me. In your materialistic world, you are faced with many distractions from the Gospel. Pray extra for your priests and bishops that they may be courageous in carrying out the duties of their office. For those who are close to Me in their prayer lives, it will go easier for them. For those who abuse their office for political and personal gain, they will have to account to Me for their misdeeds. Man is weak by sin, so your bishops need continued prayers to help lead My people."*

Later, at Adoration, I could see a dark corner with wooden sides. Jesus said: *"My people, many times you work yourself into a corner by your own habits. In order to turn around from what looks like no way out, you must change your life around and break those habits. You need to seek My grace to help you back to normal or seek someone's help. Many times you cannot do it on your own. You, yourself, have seen how the desires of your own cravings can lead you into habits of spending too much time on worldly things. When you meditate on how you waste your time, you can see more clearly that you need to prioritize your time more to do My Will. Love is a central element of following My Will. Most of your bad habits are centered around selfish desires of the mind and body. When too much of self possesses your heart, it is hard to let love of Me or your neighbor enter into your heart. The more you put love back into your life, the less these bad habits will have a hold on you. When you keep your focus on Me, you will always be able to stay on the straight and narrow road to Heaven. You may see some detours along the way, but all of these dead ends will never satisfy your soul like I can. Keep coming back to Me, no matter how many times you may be distracted."*

Wednesday, March 18, 1998:

After Communion, I could see a white outline in the form of Our Lady as was seen in some pictures. Mary said: *"My dear children, I am becoming less visible as my time of visitation draws to a close. I am coming to remind you to prepare for my feast day of the Annunciation when St. Gabriel indicated my favor with my Lord. Continue in your Lenten devotions by remembering my intentions and the Stations of the Cross. My motherly love goes out to all of my children as you prepare also for your Easter celebration. Lent and its fasting gives a somber mood, but it is necessary to prune back all of your earthly failings. Walk with me in your daily prayers, so you may draw closer to Jesus through me."*

Thursday, March 19, 1998: (St. Joseph)

After Communion, I could see St. Joseph standing with his staff. St. Joseph said: *"My dear brothers and sisters, you have heard of my lineage to David to connect the prophecy of Jesus as a son of David. Also, His mother Mary was of that same lineage. All that the Lord had foretold by His prophets had to be fulfilled in Scripture. That is why, even today, you are still following that plan of events according to the Scriptures. I had a very heavy responsibility in caring for Mary and Jesus in a hard time of conditions under the Romans. Many times the necessary traveling was difficult, but when you have a dedicated mission, the Lord provides. Those who follow a mission of teaching the Gospel have trust in the Lord for helping them in their travels and their speech. All of your lives are founded on trust and faith in Jesus that He will lead you and provide for all of your needs."*

Later, at the prayer group, I could see a light up high and a large spider web with a big spider moving down. Jesus said: *"My people, the evil one has set his snare for men and many are being trapped in his web. He leads many into electronic distractions as they are innocently drawn into temptation of sinful habits. Your new technology draws many into curiosity of new things. It is your modern idols that keep you away from adoring Me and from thanking Me for your gifts. Cast aside your desires for fame and money, for these are the sins of pride and avarice of the world."*

I could see some new shiny cars. Jesus said: *"My people, you seek the newest expensive cars, yet there will come a time when it will be difficult to fuel them. You have been humbled in having your electricity off in many places due to natural disasters. Even though your fuel is plentiful today, there will come a time when all of your new cars will not work because of evil men. Do not think that your comforts will last long. Your testing will increase with famine, disease, and pestilence."*

I could see some large factories with billows of steam coming from their stacks. Jesus said: *"My people, do not be lulled to sleep by your seemingly healthy economy. Your greed for wealth will fall in on you, as many bankruptcies will topple your markets. When you think that you are safe, riots and crime will tear you apart as a large rift will come between the rich and the poor. Since the rich fail to share their wealth, many will rise up against them in indignation. The rich will reap their harvest in tears for their ravaging of other classes."*

I could see a man in dark robes taking over the chair of St. Peter. Jesus said: *"My faithful, pray much for the Holy Father, Pope John Paul II. He is being tested dearly in his Good Friday. Many have designs to do away with him as they sought to kill Me. Once Pope John Paul II is exiled, your tribulation will begin. Events are moving quickly, even though you cannot always see what is going on. Prepare your spiritual lives to endure these persecutions."*

I could see a judge striking a gavel for order in the court. Jesus said: *"My people, your justice system has become tainted in the laws and rights that man has made. You have pushed politics into your courtrooms, where true justice is no longer possible. You let *your polls dictate reason that is far from My laws. Sin runs rampant, while justice is corrupted by money. Pray for the atonement of your sins, because the cup of My wrath is overflowing."*

I could see some large telescopes looking into the many stars of your galaxy. Jesus said: *"My people, your scientists have uncovered unusual signs in your sky and in your weather, yet few read the signs of your End Days. Why are you so blind to these happenings and still looking for signs? Many omens of your evil age have been given you, yet you fail to improve your spiritual lives. When the evil ones come, you will accept their signs, but you refuse to believe My revelations. Those who embrace the Antichrist in his illusions will loose their souls in glorifying evil instead of Me. Above all of your testing, do not be misled by this false christ. Love Me and stay faithful, and you will have your reward in My new Era of Peace."*

I could see Our Lady in blue coming to lead her children. Mary said: *"My dear children, come to me with your Rosaries and I will lead you to Jesus. Your prayer groups are powerful against the evil one and you find your comfort under my mantle of protection. Continue to gather in prayer, especially in your time of tribulation. With your sacramentals you will protect yourselves from all of the evil spirits. Call on your angels to walk with you and they will lead you to safety."*

Friday, March 20, 1998:

At St. Mary's Church of the Assumption, Santa Maria, California, I could see a Tabernacle with the Blessed Sacrament present and a hundred angels came down and separated into two columns praising Jesus. Jesus said: *"My people, wherever My Blessed Sacrament is present, there are many angels adoring My Real Presence. It is important to remember your devotions to Me in Benediction and the Stations of the Cross. Also, My Chaplet of Divine Mercy on Friday at 3:00 commemorates My death on the cross. These devotions are important to pass on to your children. How can the children know of My love, unless you bring them to Me? By your example of showing others your love for Me in your visits, you pass on these devotions to your children. Remember, I am so much a part of your life that you need to praise and honor*

Me every day of your life. The angels never tire of serving Me and adoring My Presence. If you could only have a sense of My power and how much I love you, you would do everything for Me and your heart would be filled with My endless joy."

Later, at the Cross of Peace, Santa Maria, California, during the Rosary, I could see a sporting event with some high stands and they began to crumble and fall to the ground. Mary said: *"My dear children, you will soon see your idols in sports brought low by my Son's justice. Those who let sports run their lives are making gods out of these new heroes. Ask yourself who is your master? It is in how you spend your time that you will understand who your master is. Do not let the evil one distract you, but through your prayers and persistence, you will find your peace in my Son. The things of this world will never completely satisfy you. The things of this world are not fulfilling your spirit; they leave you empty. So, seek the peace of my Son, Jesus, and you will find that He is the answer to all of your wants and desires."*

Saturday, March 21, 1998:

At the Cross of Peace Adoration, Santa Maria, California, I could see an endless stream of the faces of souls coming forward. Jesus said: *"My people, you are seeing the time for the harvest of souls where there are few in the vineyard seeking to save these souls. I am calling on My messengers and prophets to bring My Good News message to all of mankind. My End Days prophets are as the sign of Jonah which is the only sign to be given. You are being given the same message of old to prepare your souls from the evil ones by conversion and the forgiveness of sins. These messages are not new revelation, but the same call as St. John the Baptist. You have little time to prepare for the great tribulation, so heed My calls and listen to what My messengers are alerting you to. Discern the spirit for there will be false prophets, but see that time for conversion is short. Those who do not see My Coming is soon are not reading the signs of the times. I am asking everyone of My baptized faithful to reach out and bring these searching souls back to Me in love. For many are called, but few are chosen."*

Later, at the Cross of Peace, Santa Maria, California, after Communion, I could see an aisle in gold trim and people dressed in evening gowns and tuxedos. Some were walking up for awards of renown. Jesus said: *"My people, do not seek adoration and awards from men. These things are only fleeting glory and you will be forgotten tomorrow. Do not adore any of the idols of this world, but only give praise and adoration to Me. Instead of seeking awards here, seek your heavenly award to gain entrance into Heaven. To be with Me forever in sharing your crown with Me, that is the most desired award you could seek. To gain this award with Me, you must give up all of your earthly aspirations of fame and riches. Earthly fame and riches test your faith in Me. When you seek this spiritual prize, you will be like the man who sold everything to buy one precious gem. Give everything over to Me and I will grace you with eternal life in Heaven. Your love for Me will draw you above all earthly loves, because I draw your soul to its highest desire. When you love Me above all else, you will achieve the award your soul has sought from the beginning of your creation."*

Sunday, March 22, 1998:

At the Cross of Peace Adoration, Santa Maria, California, I could see a burning bush with many colors. I then saw a red color spread out all around me. God the Father said: *"I AM comes to you, My son, to show you the glory and the radiance of My love that is about to become complete over the whole world. In a short time, you will see a new era of My love make over this world into a Garden of Eden as it used to be. All evil will be cleansed from the earth. My son, tell the people how My presence is with them through My Son, Jesus' Host. When you reverence My Son, Jesus, you are respecting Me also. Come to Me, My children, as I have said to Moses and remove your shoes because you are on holy ground. Wherever My Son, Jesus' Host is present, that is holy ground. You will all be asked to preserve and protect My Blessed Sacrament. This Presence of Jesus and I will be with you in the Host until the end of time. Give glory and praise to Me for all the gifts and love I send you. Return your love to Me by your own free will and you will be blessed for giving of yourself to Me. This shining love in the bush is a sign for you of My eternal, unconditional love for all of My creatures."*

Later, at the Cross of Peace, Santa Maria, California, after Communion, I could see a pit of fire. It was a roaring inferno and there were thousands of souls falling into Hell. Jesus said: *"My people, see the souls that are falling into Hell due to their sins of rejecting Me. Pray for sinners that have cold hearts and are not loving Me. My faithful have a heavy responsibility to reach out and save as many souls as possible from going to Hell. This is your most important calling to save souls for Me. Pray and give witness of My love so that sinners may be saved. Reach out and never stop seeking even the hardest of sinners. If I do not give up on any sinner, neither should you. Struggle every day to keep your own soul protected in prayer, and then turn to help your neighbor. You are in a battle for souls between the good and evil forces. Continue your fight for souls every day. Never cease in this struggle, for Satan never sleeps and He is fighting you at every moment. Call on My help and that of your angels and the saints to carry out your work. You cannot fight this battle on your own. Solicit all of your prayer group members and all of the heavenly help and we will win the battle. Satan will be defeated. It is up to you to minimize our losses among men and women."*

Monday, March 23, 1998:

At St. Mary's Church of the Assumption, Santa Maria, California, after Communion, I could see a very ornate church, but there was an abomination of worship there. Then another very simple wooden structure was seen as a stable. An underground Mass was going on. Jesus said: *"My people, a great schism or split in My Church is coming soon. Your present churches will house a schismatic church which will deteriorate into worship of the Antichrist. The underground Masses were of My faithful remnant in simple places. You will crowd around your prayer groups to celebrate your services. As a religious persecution begins, you will have to go into hiding for your protection. There, in secret, you will hold your prayer meetings. Where there are no priests, you will call on Me in Spiritual Communion and I will come to you in the Heavenly Manna. Fear not, My people, I will always be guiding you throughout this coming trial. Have faith and trust in Me, and I will bring you to the coming Era of Peace, where you will share in a land of milk and honey."*

Tuesday, March 24, 1998:
After Communion, I followed some footprints in the sand into the water. There was a boat which I climbed into. Jesus said: *"My people, I call on all of you to follow in My footsteps and be imitators of what I have taught you. You are called also by your Baptism in the water which cleanses your sins by My Redemption. I then lead you on to the boat so you can set out on your voyage of life. During your travels, you will see storms and times of calm. Call on My help at any time, especially to weather the storms. Have trust in Me that I will bring you through everything, no matter how the evil one will taunt you. You will be able to endure your trials by the graces that I will give you. So, have no fear in life, but go forward in following My Will for you. When you follow Me in faith, you will accomplish many deeds for My glory. When you give an assent of your will to do My work, your rewards will be beyond compare. It is when you refuse My Will that you will stumble in many difficulties and confusion. Sometimes you may fall, but come back to Me in Confession. I will renew your spirit to continue your way to that sought after harbor of love in Heaven that will be at the end of your journey."*

Later, at Adoration, I could see an altar and a veil over the tabernacle in the center. I then saw a long picture of the Shroud that covered Jesus. Jesus said: *"My people, My Real Presence before you is a gift of faith to understand. If you treasure that gift, you would place Me in the center of your altars for adoration. My Image on the Shroud is a reverse image since where My radiance struck the cloth, it turned dark. This is the true image of My appearance as it was preserved on the Shroud. Your scientists analyzed the Shroud and most accounts witness to its authenticity. The details on the Shroud witness to all of My wounds that I suffered on the Cross. By examining the wounds in My hands, feet and side, you can see that I love all of you dearly to die for all mankind in this way. My sufferings were excruciating, but My pain was to save you from your sins. Give thanks for My Redemption of your souls and remember My suffering for you on Good Friday."*

Wednesday, March 25, 1998: (Feast of the Annunciation)
After Communion, I could see Mary come in a deep blue mantle with her arms stretched out and bending over to receive her children. Mary said: *"My dear children, I am happy to receive you on this my important feast day. This day the Angel Gabriel came to announce the first coming of my Son, Jesus. All Heaven and earth rejoiced that the promise of a redeemer was being fulfilled. God prepared me from birth, without sin, for this moment in time. It was an act of my will to consent to the angel's request, but this was all in God's plan from the beginning. I was always walking in the Will of God, but at that moment of my 'yes', I witnessed the Incarnation of the Son of God becoming a man. It was from that moment on that our hearts were joined as one. Be thankful for my Son, Jesus, condescending Himself into the flesh of a man. He gifted Himself for all the sins of mankind. So, come to Jesus as I have, and give your consent also to walk with Him and live as close as you can that Divine Will message He is giving to all of mankind. Receive Jesus into your hearts by emptying your heart of all of your selfish desires. When you carry your cross to Calvary, you will be preparing for his Second Coming as well."*

Thursday, March 26, 1998:
After Communion, I could see some small organisms moving around. Jesus said: *"My people, you are seeing various diseases that are going to be increasing. Some diseases will increase because of the many changes in your weather and as a consequence from disasters. Some older diseases will come back stronger with more drug resistant mutations. Another source of disease will come from germ warfare instigated by the One-World People who are creating panic in order to implement a world takeover. There are insidious people behind the scenes trying to reduce the population of the world for their own agenda. They are the same ones that are adding mutations to old diseases. Man will reap the consequences of his behavior, as world pestilence will come over the*

land. You have abused the natural order of balance in nature and you will see diseases attack in epidemics."

Later, at the prayer group, I could see a man strapped to a chair and suffering persecution. Jesus said: *"My people, a day is coming when your faith will be tested to the limit of your endurance. Evil men will taunt you and persecute you for believing in My Name. Some may be faced with martyrdom instead of giving up their faith. Evil people will torture you and try to make an example of you to cast fear into the believers. I tell you to lift your head up high and never deny Me, no matter if they even threaten to take your life. If you love Me, you will go this extra mile for Me. The Holy Spirit will strengthen you and speak for you. You may suffer for a time, but your glory will be known throughout Heaven."*

I could see some old statues of civilizations long ago. Jesus said: *"My people, throughout history My Words of love in the Scriptures have caused many to refuse to accept My ways. Many do not want to give up their will to follow Me. They lust for their comforts and pleasures. It is not easy to live a life of a Christian. They have criticized and crucified Me because they did not want to give everything up for Me. I offer My love and peace in Heaven, but you will be rejected by men as I was."*

I could see a bright light on some people on a porch and darkness was all around them. Jesus said: *"My people, live in My light of faith always eager to shine your love on others. Those who accept Me are not afraid to reveal their deeds before Me and man. Those wicked souls want to keep their deeds in the darkness, so no one can see how evil they are. Their souls have a high price that may require much prayer and patience to save them."*

I could see a bright flame in the darkness. Jesus said: *"You, My people, need to be a beacon of light for those souls that you are trying to save. I am the eternal and ever-vigilant light that speaks to your hearts. It is the light of My Word in the Scriptures that draws you to Me. It is the fire of love from the Holy Spirit that will ignite love in your soul. Stay close to Me so the warmth of My love will give you heavenly comfort."*

I could see and feel the pain of loss in the latest killings by the young boys. Jesus said: *"My people, this latest tragedy has caused many to question how this could happen. This is an extension of how society's permissiveness has allowed a mentality of killing to be even contemplated. Many children are not being taught about sin or things they cannot do. Life has a low price, when killing by abortion and mercy killing are accepted. Violence on TV and in life have shown children the wrong incentives. Love and a high regard for life is missing in your families. These actions are a reflection of society's failure to establish proper moral formation in the children. Struggle in prayer and good example to train your children before they are out of control."*

I could see a poor black family in Africa. Jesus said: *"My people, take note of the poverty and helplessness of these poor hungry souls. Do not turn your back on your fellow men and women, but reach out to help them in your own way. If you turn away from helping them, you turn your face from Me. Do not just give lip service to their plight, but do whatever you can to feed and clothe them. They need your help and you should be willing to share a portion of your abundant gifts with them."*

I could see some twirling columns of wind. Jesus said: *"My people, you have been faced with a whirlwind of events occurring one on top of the other. Through your media you are being bombarded every day with violence in your weather and in your killings. The morals of your society are reaching such a low point that your civilization stands on the brink of ruin. Where sins of the flesh are not even deemed evil, how can your children be protected? It is your lifestyles of wanton sex and homosexuality that will be your downfall. Unless you accept yourselves as sinners and reform your lives, you will have to suffer My wrath as the angels will separate the wheat from the tares."*

Friday, March 27, 1998:

After Communion, I could see a white and black nurse with masks over their faces. Jesus said: *"My people, you will see a day coming soon when air-born diseases will travel quickly over many people. There will come such epidemics that there will not be enough medicine to stop this sickness. Some of these epidemics will be started by germ warfare. Isolation from the sick will be your only defense. As the time of the tribulation arrives, this will be another reason to go into hiding. At the safe havens and caves, all of your sicknesses will be miraculously cured. As the pestilence of famine and disease spreads over the land, these places of My protection will be sought by many of My faithful. Have faith and trust in My help and you will have everything provided for you."*

Later, at St. Elizabeth Ann Seton Church, Fort Wayne, Indiana, after Communion, I could see a large sword over an altar and then a vision of an Arab man in a turban. Jesus said: *"My people, I am showing the sword of the Arabs that is being lifted against My people and My Church. It is the Arab leaders that are leading a holy war against the Israelites and the Christians. Their anger against My people is like the anger of those who came with swords and clubs to crucify Me. The anger towards Me and My followers has continued to this day. Pray, My people, for all of your persecutors, even the ones wanting to take your life. As I told St. Peter to put back his sword in My defense, so I ask My faithful to not lift arms against your enemies. Let your love radiate out to everyone, so you may influence others and bring this world closer to My peace. This peace, you pray for, may require your life to demonstrate your love of God and neighbor. You may see some martyred, but in the end it is My Will that will prevail over men."*

Saturday, March 28, 1998:

At St. Jude's Church, Fort Wayne, Indiana, after Communion, I could see a little creek which went on further into a stream and finally into a river. Jesus said: *"My people, during your Lenten journey, I wish to share with you in My living water. As I told the woman at the well, I will provide My living water of Baptism that one will drink and never again thirst. Those who are Baptized are given a faith that will never die as long as they are spiritually nourished. I give My healing waters in Confession. All of My sacraments give you My graces to carry on in your spiritual lives. It is when you experience a daily growth in your faith, that you are gaining in your perfection. Reach out to Me each day that I may lead you in your faith walk of love of God and love of neighbor. The body needs water to survive, but I supply the living water of My grace that keeps your spirit alive in Me. Be joyful and*

Prepare for the Great Tribulation and the Era of Peace

J.   T.

rejoice in My abundant graces where you are always showered with My infinite love."

Later, at St. Jude's Adoration, Fort Wayne, Indiana, I could see the Holy Stairs in Rome. These were the steps to Pilate at the condemnation of Jesus. Jesus said: *"My people, as you look on these stairs, you see the significance as Passion Week draws closer. I walked these steps to My judgment with Pilate. You also will have to approach the stairs to your own judgment, as you come to the Gates of Heaven. I have suffered for your sins. So, when you face the Father, your ransom has already been paid. Many make a practice of climbing the stairs on their knees. The more reparation for sin you do on earth, the less you will have to do in Purgatory. As you see My love in offering My life for you, you in return can give your will over to Me. Prepare in your prayers for Holy Week when you will relive My Crucifixion. Lent will be concluding shortly, so use your time wisely in your own devotions. You commemorate My death at every Mass, so take note of all the readings which enrich this season. You will then be joyful soon, as you celebrate My Resurrection on Easter Sunday. Rejoice, because you will soon see your Easter Sunday in the Era of Peace after your Good Friday of the tribulation."*

Sunday, March 29, 1998: (Ashley and Drew's First Communion) At St. Elizabeth Ann Seton Church, Fort Wayne, Indiana, after Communion, I could see a large gem wrapped in a beautiful holder on the altar. Jesus said: *"My people, the prize of Heaven is always among you in My Real Presence in the Eucharist. Every time you receive Me in Holy Communion, you receive a little taste of Heaven. When you come to Heaven, you will be in this same ecstasy for all eternity. My Real Presence is your heaven on earth in every tabernacle all over the earth. For those who adore Me and treasure My Real Presence among them come and visit Me in adoration. Celebrate My joy with you in the quiet of your heart. Bring the little children to Me, so they can experience My love in Holy Communion as well. Teach your children the faith that you have been gifted with. My love is to be shared with all ages and all peoples. I am King of the Universe and worthy of your praise. I draw all of you to My Eucharistic Banquet at the Mass and also to the great banquet of the faithful in Heaven with all of the angels and saints. Rejoice that your Lord loves you so much that I died for you on the Cross. Keep your souls cleansed of your sins in Confession so you can receive Me often."*

Prepare for the Great Tribulation and the Era of Peace

Monday, March 30, 1998:
At St. John the Evangelist Church after Communion I could see a pillar of stone in the darkness and then a kneeler in a church. Jesus said: *"My people, many times you are feeling down either from the difficulties of life or the dreariness of a long winter. When spring comes with the flowers, longer days, and warmer weather, you become invigorated and uplifted. For souls deep in the darkness of sin, I am the light of your soul calling you to forgiveness. When you come out of Confession, you are infused with My grace and love and you feel released from your sins. A spiritual dawn of new light now enters your soul as you share in the lifting of your burden from your shoulders. Do not let the guilt and confusion of sin destroy your peace, but reach out to Me in Confession to have your spirit renewed and replenished with My love. The joy of a freshly forgiven soul is beyond compare. For you were lost and now you are found. You have strayed from your path to Me, and now I have set you aright toward Heaven once again. This spiritual cleansing is the best spring cleaning you could profit from."*

Later, at Adoration, I could see a long wooden building as a church in the night. Then I saw a fire start at the rear of the church and it burned down completely. Jesus said: *"My people, you will soon be tested by a schism in My Church where your churches will be taken over by those against Pope John Paul II. This is why I am preparing My remnant to support those priests who will still follow the true teachings of My Church. You must prepare now so you can provide places in your prayer groups for underground Masses. Provide the needed vessels and the unleavened bread and wine. The later stages of religious persecution will come as many of your churches will be destroyed or used for other purposes. It is when they come to put you in detention centers for belief in Me, that you will have to flee your homes into hiding. They will hunt you down as the armies of Hitler persecuted and killed the Jews. During the tribulation of the Antichrist you will be surviving by trusting in My help to protect your souls. With faith in Me, you will save your souls as I conquer all evil spirits and evil men."*

Tuesday, March 31, 1998:

After Communion, I could see some large lights up very high in an auditorium. Jesus said: *"My son, I have called you to go out and preach the word of My Gospel, and to prepare the people for the coming events. The warning messages I have given you are not an easy message to give, yet it is what I am asking of you. You have been gracious with your time and willing to do My Will. This will not be required of you much longer, since events will occur to keep you from speaking out publicly. So, I am asking you to continue while you can, for many souls are reaching out for the sacred, but they are not being fed by those who should be spreading My Word. This is the reason that I have called many messengers at this time to feed the people the warmth of My love and the knowledge of things to come. Listen and heed the true messages given and My faithful will be directed how to make way for My coming again."*

Later, at Adoration, I could see a massive blue light that beamed up from the earth and at the top was a gold object. Jesus said: *"My people, be prepared when the Antichrist comes claiming to be Me. I have told you not to believe in any false witness that claims to be Me, no matter what signs and miracles he may demonstrate. Even if he should show miraculous signs in the sky or any other illusions, do not believe in him. Believe in Me only and do not be misled. He will try to do anything to get you to worship him. Refuse any chips in your hand, and do not watch this Antichrist on TV since he may influence your minds. He will have mind control over many people through electrical devices. Keep fixed on Me as your Savior and have faith that I will protect you from this evil one. Pray to your guardian angels to have them lead you to safety."*

Prepare for the Great Tribulation and the Era of Peace

Index

Volume X

abortion
   for convenience & luxury (Jesus) — 1/22/98
   new executioners (Jesus) — 2/6/98
   sold like Jesus (Jesus) — 3/13/98
   thirty pieces of silver (Mary) — 3/5/98
   weather,disease are testings (Jesus) — 3/13/98
   weighs against US (Jesus) — 1/22/98
abortion clinic
   closed across from image (Mary) — 2/28/98
activities
   we race too much (Jesus) — 2/14/98
Adam
   live as in New Era (Jesus) — 1/10/98
Adam and Eve
   banished from garden (Jesus) — 1/31/98
Adam's sin
   born to die (Jesus) — 1/11/98
America
   will collapse from its decay (Jesus) — 2/25/98
angels
   difficult to help in serious sin (St. Michael) — 2/26/98
   lead to safe havens (Jesus) — 2/13/98
   lead you for protection (Jesus) — 2/5/98
   protect us in our work (Jesus) — 3/15/98
   serve and adore God (Jesus) — 3/20/98
   strength in end days (Mary) — 1/1/98
annihilation of nations
   pray to stop (Mary) — 2/19/98
Annunciation
   God's favor (Mary) — 3/18/98
Antichrist
   and One World People (Jesus) — 2/6/98
   churches closed,burned (Jesus) — 1/11/98
   declaration amidst chaos (Jesus) — 2/10/98
   declaration triggered (Jesus) — 2/19/98
   do not believe illusions (Jesus) — 3/19/98
   do not follow him (Jesus) — 2/28/98
   empty promises (Jesus) — 2/1/98
   faithful outlawed (Jesus) — 1/5/98
   illusions, TV, control (Jesus) — 3/31/98
   justice falling on his reign (Jesus) — 3/5/98
   refuse chips (Jesus) — 3/31/98
   rule in financial collapse (Jesus) — 3/5/98
   technology in place for (Jesus) — 1/25/98
   test signs in the sky (Jesus) — 1/30/98
Antipope
   and Antichrist dominate (Jesus) — 2/5/98
apostasy
   as tribulation approaches (Jesus) — 2/13/98
Arabs
   leading a holy war (Jesus) — 3/27/98
Armageddon
   birds pick carcasses (Jesus) — 2/9/98
   mother of all battles (Jesus) — 2/19/98
   running in reckless abandon (Jesus) — 1/27/98
astrology
   do not be influenced (Jesus) — 1/2/98
Audrey Santos
   preciousness of life (Mary) — 1/15/98
   suffering servant (Jesus) — 1/14/98
Baptism
   cleanses your sins (Jesus) — 3/24/98
   our call to ministry (Jesus) — 1/11/98
   the living water (Jesus) — 3/28/98
battle of good and evil
   armor of faith and trust (Jesus) — 2/8/98
Bible
   read daily (Jesus) — 1/1/98
bishops and priests
   pray for them (Jesus) — 3/17/98
blackouts
   Canada and U.S. (Jesus) — 1/25/98
bleeding Hosts
   raise our faith (Jesus) — 1/15/98
Blessed Mother Mary
   messages ending (Mary) — 2/5/98

Prepare for the Great Tribulation and the Era of Peace

Blessed Sacrament	
adoration-reward in Heaven (Jesus)	3/6/98
give proper respect (Jesus)	3/13/98
give thanks & praise (Jesus)	1/18/98
real presence (Jesus)	2/27/98
burning bush	
sign of eternal love (God the Father)	3/22/98
Calvary	
desert of Lent to (Jesus)	3/16/98
Canada	
punishment in ice storm (Jesus)	1/15/98
caves	
best protection (Jesus)	1/27/98
protect in nuclear war (Jesus)	2/19/98
protection in tribulation (Mary)	1/16/98
charity	
give of substance (Jesus)	3/3/98
chastisements	
rain sign of cleansing (Jesus)	1/9/98
children	
great responsibility for faith (Jesus)	3/8/98
moral formation of (Jesus)	3/26/98
take to Mass & Adoration (St. Therese)	3/3/98
teach the faith (Jesus)	2/21/98
choose	
direction in life (Jesus)	3/12/98
choose life	
stop wars & abortions (Jesus)	2/5/98
Clearwater, Florida	
miraculous image (Mary)	2/28/98
Clinton	
will answer to God (Jesus)	1/23/98
comets & asteroids	
collisions on earth (Jesus)	3/14/98
Confession	
be prepared to die (Jesus)	3/9/98
contrition and forgiveness (Jesus)	2/15/98
light of our soul (Jesus)	3/30/98
necessary for salvation (Jesus)	1/15/98
restore to grace (Jesus)	1/8/98
seek true forgiveness (God the Father)	2/22/98
spirit renewed (Jesus)	1/13/98
spiritual spring cleaning (Jesus)	3/30/98
conversion	
fight the good fight (St. Therese)	1/9/98
corporal works of mercy	
prove your love for God (Jesus)	2/20/98
corporate cutbacks	
help jobless (Jesus)	1/22/98
creation	
by the Master Builder (Jesus)	2/2/98
crucifix	
protection from evil spirits (Jesus)	3/12/98
crucifixes	
display as remembrance (Jesus)	1/22/98
show Divine sacrifice (Jesus)	2/20/98
Cuba	
Pope brought love (Jesus)	1/23/98
David	
pray for intercession (David)	1/8/98
death	
immortality of soul (Jesus)	2/18/98
prepare with Confession (Jesus)	2/23/98
death culture	
readied for tribulation (Jesus)	2/12/98
decisions	
accept our responsibility (Jesus)	2/7/98
decisions in life	
base on Divine Will (Jesus)	1/29/98
demons	
come from volcanoes (Jesus)	3/12/98
detention centers	
take prisoners to (Jesus)	2/5/98
devil	
do not give him credit (Jesus)	2/7/98
devotions	
chaplet,stations,adoration (Jesus)	3/20/98
disasters	
help each other (Jesus)	2/12/98
stripped of comforts (Jesus)	2/12/98
to get our attention (Jesus)	3/10/98
war, famine, pestilence (Jesus)	2/5/98
by man and nature (Jesus)	3/12/98

cured at safe havens,caves (Jesus)	3/27/98		eternal now	
from disasters and weather (Jesus)	3/26/98		prepare soul by Confession (Jesus)	2/18/98
distractions			Eucharist	
pray to clear mind (Jesus)	2/24/98		greatest gift FREE (Jesus)	2/14/98
spiritual reading (Jesus)	1/1/98		until the end of time (Jesus)	1/11/98
Divine Will			evangelize	
do not want to give up to (Jesus)	3/26/98		call to save souls important (Jesus)	3/22/98
gain crown (Jesus)	1/3/98		highest calling (Jesus)	3/2/98
keep focused on Jesus (Jesus)	1/7/98		live the Gospel (St. Therese)	2/7/98
live close to (Mary)	3/25/98		quickly (Jesus)	2/5/98
doorway to Heaven			rejoice to save souls (Jesus)	1/8/98
miraculous pictures (Jesus)	1/19/98		times have not changed (Jesus)	1/10/98
Easter duty			events	
go to Confession (Jesus)	3/4/98		occurring very fast (Jesus)	1/25/98
eclipse			evil	
a whirlwind of events (Jesus)	2/19/98		allowed as a test (Jesus)	2/19/98
sign of dramatic events (Jesus)	1/29/98		evil one	
eclipses and asteroids			more attacks as souls saved (Jesus)	2/20/98
omens of things to come (Jesus)	3/12/98		evil spirits	
economy			holy water,sacramentals (Jesus)	3/5/98
bankruptcies,markets to fall (Jesus)	3/19/98		faith	
rich demand more profits (Jesus)	1/29/98		endurance in (Jesus)	2/4/98
electronic devices			to overcome all evil (Jesus)	2/17/98
run our lives (Jesus)	2/14/98		faithful	
electronics			do not grieve in death (Jesus)	1/3/98
distractions of evil (Jesus)	3/19/98		families	
end days			seek peace most (Mary)	3/12/98
fulfilled in Revelation (Jesus)	2/2/98		fasting	
fulfillment of Scripture (Jesus)	1/25/98		train body and soul (Jesus)	2/23/98
end times			Feast of Annunciation	
lie at the door (Jesus)	2/5/98		Mary gave her 'yes' (Mary)	3/25/98
entertainment			food	
poisoning children's minds (Jesus)	3/2/98		prepare some (Jesus)	2/5/98
environment			food preparation	
storms caused by abuse (Jesus)	2/12/98		for disasters (Jesus)	1/22/98
war and pollution (Jesus)	2/13/98		free will	
Era of Peace			of man and angels (Jesus)	2/2/98
evil conquered, new earth (Jesus)	3/5/98		fuel	
land of milk and honey (Jesus)	3/23/98		in short supply (Jesus)	3/19/98
our Easter Sunday (Jesus)	3/28/98		gasoline	
radiant bodies (Jesus)	1/31/98		endangered in war (Jesus)	1/25/98

Prepare for the Great Tribulation and the Era of Peace

George Albert
   a witness of faith (Jesus) — 3/12/98
germ warfare
   of One World (Jesus) — 3/26/98
   start epidemics (Jesus) — 3/27/98
gift of life
   treasure love and life (Jesus) — 2/3/98
God the Father
   worthy of worship (God the Father) — 2/22/98
Gospel
   power of His Word (Jesus) — 2/8/98
   put into practice (Jesus) — 1/18/98
gossip
   curb your tongue (Jesus) — 1/26/98
governments
   not stable much longer (Jesus) — 2/5/98
guardian angels
   keep close (Jesus) — 1/2/98
   protection of (Jesus) — 1/13/98
handicapped
   help physically,spiritually (Jesus) — 1/22/98
harvest of souls
   time is short (Jesus) — 3/21/98
healing
   physically & spiritually (Jesus) — 1/18/98
healings
   spiritual and physical (Mary) — 2/11/98
   spiritual,physical,mind (Jesus) — 2/3/98
heaven on earth
   reward for labors (Jesus) — 1/6/98
helicopters
   more active roll (Jesus) — 3/12/98
Hell
   many souls falling into (Jesus) — 3/22/98
hiding
   protection of angels (Jesus) — 3/12/98
   to escape diseases (Jesus) — 3/27/98
Holy Communion
   union of spirits (Jesus) — 3/7/98
holy ground
   cure ills,provide manna (Jesus) — 1/13/98
   presence in Host (God the Father) — 3/22/98

Holy Shroud
   energy flashed the image (Jesus) — 3/15/98
Holy Spirit
   be baptized in (Jesus) — 1/8/98
   gives life (Holy Spirit) — 1/14/98
   help in speaking (Holy Spirit) — 1/14/98
   infinite love by (Jesus) — 1/8/98
   power of peace & love (Jesus) — 1/13/98
   protect souls with love (Jesus) — 3/12/98
   will strengthen,speak for you (Jesus) — 3/26/98
Holy Stairs
   Jesus' steps to Pilate (Jesus) — 3/28/98
homosexuality and sex
   is our downfall (Jesus) — 3/26/98
Hussein
   pray for leaders (Jesus) — 2/9/98
   weapons hidden in hills (Jesus) — 2/12/98
ice storm
   in Canada (Jesus) — 1/15/98
Incarnation
   hearts as one (Mary) — 3/25/98
innocent victims
   help with alms (Jesus) — 2/26/98
Iraq
   miscalculated war (Jesus) — 1/30/98
   One World Order and oil (Jesus) — 1/28/98
   took liberties with weakness (Jesus) — 1/25/98
Iraq war
   make problems worse (Jesus) — 2/17/98
   our troops stretched thin (Jesus) — 2/6/98
   quagmire of trouble (Jesus) — 2/15/98
Ireland
   shared faith experience (Jesus) — 3/15/98
jobs
   feel like prisoners (Jesus) — 1/7/98
   lower standard of living (Jesus) — 2/12/98
Joe Trunfio
   witness of faith (Jesus) — 2/24/98
judging
   spiritually & physically (Jesus) — 1/4/98

judgment
    huge price for killers (Jesus) — 2/6/98
    stand in His Light (Jesus) — 1/15/98
judgment day
    reunited with body (Jesus) — 2/18/98
judgments
    only God judges (Jesus) — 1/26/98
justice system
    collapse with injustices (Jesus) — 3/7/98
    corrupted by money (Jesus) — 3/19/98
    not true justice (Jesus) — 2/26/98
killing
    arrogance of power (Jesus) — 2/6/98
King of the Universe
    give glory and praise (Jesus) — 1/4/98
    He guides everything (Jesus) — 3/12/98
King of Universe
    worthy of praise (Jesus) — 3/29/98
knowledge increase
    sign of end times (Jesus) — 3/8/98
Lamb of God
    saved by Precious Blood (Jesus) — 1/10/98
lawyers
    greed for money (Jesus) — 2/26/98
leaders
    pray for spiritual & secular (Jesus) — 1/20/98
    pray to have peace (Jesus) — 2/26/98
leisure time
    who is your master? (Mary) — 3/20/98
Lent
    desert experience (Jesus) — 2/23/98
    prayer and self-denial (Jesus) — 2/26/98
    prune earthly failings (Mary) — 3/18/98
    prune occasions of sin (Jesus) — 3/4/98
    renew spiritual lives (Jesus) — 3/2/98
    suffer as Jesus (Jesus) — 3/16/98
life cycle
    here a short time (Jesus) — 3/9/98
love
    call on Jesus for help (Jesus) — 1/27/98
    central to Divine Will (Jesus) — 3/17/98
    focus on His joy (Jesus) — 1/15/98

    Jesus cries tears of (Jesus) — 1/17/98
    unconditional & infinite (Jesus) — 1/12/98
manna
    angels bring Communion (Jesus) — 2/8/98
    angels will provide (Jesus) — 2/14/98
    in Real Presence (Jesus) — 2/19/98
    Spiritual Communion (Jesus) — 1/12/98
Mark of the Beast
    do not take it (Jesus) — 1/5/98
Marmora
    holy ground place (Mary) — 2/22/98
martyrdom
    prophets persecuted (Jesus) — 1/14/98
    to stay faithful (Jesus) — 3/26/98
Mass
    preserve proper words (Jesus) — 2/19/98
Masses
    remnant in underground (Jesus) — 1/12/98
    valid and invalid (Jesus) — 1/8/98
materialism
    selfishness & control (Jesus) — 1/6/98
    will be stripped of things (Jesus) — 3/9/98
messages
    about to end for Mary (Mary) — 1/1/98
    act on them daily (Jesus) — 2/4/98
    by Mary to stop (Mary) — 2/5/98
messengers
    feed the people (Jesus) — 3/31/98
    prepare for tribulation (Jesus) — 3/21/98
Mid-East war
    destruction, no winners (Jesus) — 1/29/98
monasteries
    safe havens (Jesus) — 1/13/98
mortal sin
    lose light of grace (Jesus) — 1/16/98
movies and TV
    corruption of society (Jesus) — 2/11/98
Mystical Body
    all share in pain (Jesus) — 2/12/98
    reflection of Jesus (Jesus) — 2/9/98
    unite in love (Jesus) — 1/5/98

Prepare for the Great Tribulation and the Era of Peace

nature	
abused balance of (Jesus)	3/26/98
neighbors	
reach out in love (Jesus)	3/15/98
New Age Movement	
evil signs & illusions (Jesus)	1/2/98
New Age symbols	
Satanic sacramentals (Jesus)	3/5/98
new earth	
follow Divine Will (Jesus)	2/2/98
New Era	
radiance of His love (God the Father)	3/22/98
New Jerusalem	
final preparation for Heaven (God the Father)	2/22/98
nuclear war	
pray to mitigate (Jesus)	2/19/98
wasteland on earth (Jesus)	1/27/98
oil	
fuel threatened (Jesus)	1/19/98
oiling statues	
raise our faith (Jesus)	1/15/98
Olympic Games	
love in family of nations (Jesus)	1/15/98
One World Order	
reduce population (Jesus)	3/26/98
One World People	
are using Clinton (Jesus)	1/23/98
involved in war (Jesus)	2/9/98
world war takeover (Jesus)	2/1/98
original sin	
be baptized into Light (Jesus)	1/13/98
Our Lady of Guadalupe	
image on building (Mary)	2/28/98
perfection	
purified in fire (Jesus)	2/10/98
persecution	
forced to flee (Jesus)	3/7/98
in underground Masses (Jesus)	2/19/98
never deny Jesus in (Jesus)	3/26/98
test of faith (Jesus)	2/9/98
underground Church (Jesus)	1/2/98
police state	
to prevent terrorism (Jesus)	3/7/98
poor people	
everyone's responsibility (Jesus)	1/29/98
give help (Mary)	1/22/98
help with prayers, money (Jesus)	1/22/98
share and help with them (Jesus)	3/2/98
Pope John Paul II	
example of evangelization (Jesus)	1/23/98
exiled, tribulation begins (Jesus)	3/19/98
follow him & Magisterium (Jesus)	2/28/98
give prayer support (Mary)	1/8/98
last faithful pope (Jesus)	2/5/98
poverty	
reach out to help (Jesus)	3/26/98
power outages	
more frequent (Jesus)	1/8/98
praise and glory	
seek God first (Jesus)	3/10/98
prayer	
make time for (Jesus)	2/24/98
Rosary and scapular (Mary)	1/1/98
prayer groups	
to endure persecution (Jesus)	2/26/98
to fight battle (Jesus)	3/22/98
very powerful (Mary)	3/19/98
prayer warriors	
fight the good fight (Jesus)	1/3/98
prayers	
good intentions count (Jesus)	1/24/98
pride	
the root of other sins (Jesus)	1/24/98
pride and privacy	
tear down walls to neighbor (Jesus)	3/15/98
priorities	
do not be selfish (Jesus)	1/4/98
Prodigal Son, The	
Heaven rejoices (Jesus)	3/14/98
prophets and saints	
given miraculous help (Jesus)	1/21/98
Purgatory	
do reparation here (Jesus)	3/28/98

suffer now or later (Jesus)	1/12/98	scales of justice	
temporal punishment (Jesus)	1/31/98	on side of evil (Jesus)	1/29/98
Real Presence		schism	
our prize of Heaven (Jesus)	3/29/98	hide from persecution (Jesus)	3/23/98
Reconciliation		money & social events (Jesus)	1/12/98
graces for salvation (Jesus)	3/1/98	underground Masses (Jesus)	2/8/98
religious education		underground Masses (Jesus)	1/11/98
teach children (Jesus)	3/8/98	schools	
remnant		do not take God out (Jesus)	2/25/98
in underground Masses (Jesus)	3/23/98	scientist	
led by John Paul II (Jesus)	2/8/98	analyzes the Shroud (Jesus)	3/24/98
protected, real presence (Jesus)	1/11/98	Scripture	
renewal of earth		must be fulfilled (St. Joseph)	3/19/98
restore order (Jesus)	1/27/98	Scriptures	
renewed earth		fulfilled by Jesus (Jesus)	1/8/98
faithful will see (Jesus)	1/2/98	Light of His Word (Jesus)	3/26/98
Resurrection		Second Coming	
a witness for us (Jesus)	1/11/98	on clouds of glory (Jesus)	1/30/98
of our bodies and souls (Jesus)	3/15/98	selfishness	
rites		help those in need (Jesus)	1/29/98
have same true God (Jesus)	2/27/98	no room for God (Jesus)	3/11/98
Rosary		Shroud of Turin	
15 decades for peace (Mary)	2/19/98	His true image and love (Jesus)	3/24/98
sacramentals		signs in the sky	
to fight the battle (Mark)	3/12/98	people still will not believe (Jesus)	3/19/98
sacraments		spinning sun (Jesus)	1/30/98
free from sin (Jesus)	1/15/98	Simeon's prophecy	
safety		Our Lady's sorrows (Mary)	2/2/98
angels and sacramentals (Mary)	3/19/98	sin	
saints		responsible for actions (Jesus)	3/6/98
call by name for help (St. Therese)	2/7/98	sins	
keep statues to remember (Jesus)	2/26/98	Jesus continues to suffer (Jesus)	1/12/98
removed from churches (Jesus)	1/12/98	society	
salvation		bring order or collapse (Jesus)	2/12/98
recognize we are sinners (Jesus)	2/1/98	mentality of killing (Jesus)	3/26/98
Satan		on brink of ruin (Jesus)	3/26/98
be on guard, he never sleeps (Jesus)	1/26/98	seeks instant gratification (Jesus)	1/29/98
little time left (Jesus)	1/9/98	souls	
never sleeps (Jesus)	3/22/98	some have a high price (Jesus)	3/26/98
stirring up war (Jesus)	2/5/98	sponsors	
war of destruction (Jesus)	2/12/98	are blessed in this work (Jesus)	3/15/98

Prepare for the Great Tribulation and the Era of Peace

sports
    idols brought low (Mary) — 3/20/98
St. Joseph
    lineage of David (St. Joseph) — 3/19/98
St. Michael
    guardian of U.S. (St. Michael) — 2/26/98
St. Peter
    put back the sword (Jesus) — 3/27/98
storms
    abortions & sins of the flesh (Jesus) — 1/29/98
    chastisement for sins (Jesus) — 3/5/98
    sins need cleansing (Jesus) — 2/19/98
    strip possessions (Jesus) — 1/20/98
suffering
    a grace to be stronger (Jesus) — 1/10/98
    daily crosses (Mary) — 2/2/98
    the price for souls (Jesus) — 3/5/98
tabernacles
    to places of disrespect (Jesus) — 1/12/98
talents
    use for God and neighbor (Jesus) — 2/16/98
technology
    creation being abused (Jesus) — 3/8/98
temporal punishment
    due to sin (Jesus) — 1/31/98
terrorists
    risk lives (Jesus) — 1/8/98
The Holy Family
    unite families in love (Jesus) — 1/15/98
toxic weapons
    put poisons in the air (Jesus) — 2/19/98
traditions
    restore & preserve (Jesus) — 1/13/98
Transfiguration
    Mystery of Trinity (Jesus) — 1/31/98
trials
    endured by His graces (Jesus) — 3/24/98
tribulation
    angels will help (Mark) — 3/12/98
    can start any time (Mark) — 3/12/98
    demons roam the earth (Jesus) — 2/17/98
    like a train in a tunnel (Jesus) — 1/6/98
    signs of it to begin (Jesus) — 2/10/98
Trinity
    in consecrated Host (Holy Spirit) — 1/14/98
    mystery of faith (Jesus) — 2/7/98
Triumph
    before man destroys self (Jesus) — 2/12/98
    sooner than asteroid (Mark) — 3/12/98
trust and faith
    help in mission (St. Joseph) — 3/19/98
United Nations
    to take us over (Jesus) — 2/6/98
United States
    founded on God (Jesus) — 2/12/98
volcanoes
    increased activity (Jesus) — 3/12/98
war
    Mid-East area (Jesus) — 1/19/98
    pray for peace (Jesus) — 2/16/98
    prayers gave reprieve (Mary) — 3/12/98
    pride of leaders seek (Jesus) — 2/26/98
    will not settle disputes (Jesus) — 1/8/98
warning
    all will know who God is (God the Father) — 2/22/98
    wake up from complacency (Jesus) — 1/25/98
Warning messages
    personal mission (Jesus) — 3/31/98
water
    contaminated in war (Jesus) — 2/19/98
    miraculous springs (Mary) — 1/16/98
weapons of mass killing
    destroy all life (Jesus) — 2/12/98
weather
    food shortages & disease (Jesus) — 2/26/98
    storms increase, sin (Jesus) — 1/8/98
    will affect movie industry (Jesus) — 3/2/98
women
    role models of faith (Jesus) — 3/5/98
world depression
    greed of the rich (Jesus) — 3/5/98
world war
    pray not to start (Jesus) — 2/5/98

Volume X

Prepare for the Great Tribulation and the Era of Peace

Volume X

More Messages from God through John Leary

If you would like to take advantage of more precious words from Jesus and Mary and apply them to your lives, read the first three volumes of messages and visions given to us through John's special gift. Each book contains a full year of daily messages and visions. As Jesus and Mary said in volume IV:

Listen to My words of warning, and you will be ready to share in the beauty of the Second Coming. Jesus 7/4/96

I will work miracles of conversion on those who read these books with an open mind. Jesus 9/5/96

Prepare for the Great Tribulation and the Era of Peace

Volume I - *Messages received from July 1993 to June 1994*
ISBN# 1-882972-69-4 256pp. - $7.95

Volume II - *Messages received from July 1994 to June 1995*
ISBN# 1 882972-72-4 352pp. - $8.95

Volume III - *Messages received from July 1995 to July 10, 1996*
ISBN# 1-882972-77-5 384pp. - $8.95

Volume IV - *Messages received from July 11, 1996 to Sept. 30, 1996*
ISBN# 1-882972-91-0 104pp. - $2.95

Volume V - *Messages received from Oct. 1, 1996 to Dec. 31, 1996*
ISBN# 1-882972-97-X 120pp. - $2.95

Volume VI - *Messages received from Jan. 1, 1997 to Mar. 31, 1997*
ISBN# 1-57918-002-7 112pp. - $2.95

Volume VII - *Messages received from April 1, 1997 to June 30, 1997*
ISBN# 1-57918-010-8 112pp. - $2.95

Volume VIII - *Messages received from July 1, 1997 to September 30, 1997*
ISBN# 1-57918-053-1 128pp. - $3.95

Volume IX - *Messages received from Oct. 1, 1997 to Dec. 30, 1997*
ISBN# 1-57918-066-3 168pp. - $3.95

Other Great Titles From
QUEENSHIP PUBLISHING
From your local Catholic bookstore or direct from the Publisher

Trial, Tribulation and Triumph
Before, During and After Antichrist
Desmond Birch
ISBN# 1-882972-73-2 $19.50

The Amazing Secret of the Souls in Purgatory
An Interview with Maria Simma
Sr. Emmanuel of Medjugorje
ISBN# 1-57918-004-3 $4.95

After the Darkness
A Catholic Novel on the Coming of the Antichrist and the End of the World
Rev. Joseph M. Esper
ISBN# 1-57918-048-5 $14.95

Mary's Three Gifts to Her Beloved Priests
A Deeper Understanding of Our Lady's Messages to Fr. Gobbi
Rev. Albert Shamon
ISBN# 1-57918-005-1 $2.95

The Final Warning
And a Defense Against Modernism
Paul A. Mihalik, Sr., Lt. Colonel USAF (Ret.)
ISBN# 1-57918-043-4 $4.95

A Light Shone in the Darkness
The Story of the Stigmatist and Mystic Therese Neumann of Konnersreuth
Doreen Mary Rossman
ISBN# 1-57918-044-2 $12.95

A Little Catechism on the Holy Rosary
Miguel Guadalupe
ISBN# 1-882972-78-3 $4.95

Call of the Ages
The Apparitions and Revelations of the Virgin Mary Foretell the Coming of Evil and an Era of Peace
Thomas W. Petrisko
ISBN# 1-882972-59-7 $11.95